T0023662

THE **MINI** ROUGH GUIDE TO
CRETE

YOUR TAILOR-MADE TRIP
STARTS HERE

Tailor-made trips and unique adventures crafted by local experts

Rough Guides has been inspiring travellers for more than 35 years. Leave it to our local experts to create your perfect itinerary and book it at local rates.

Don't follow the crowd – find your own path.

HOW ROUGHGUIDES.COM/TRIPS WORKS

STEP 1 Pick your dream destination, tell us what you want and submit an enquiry.

STEP 2 Fill in a short form to tell your local expert about your dream trip and preferences.

STEP 3 Our local expert will craft your tailor-made itinerary. You'll be able to tweak and refine it until you're completely satisfied.

STEP 4 Book online with ease, pack your bags and enjoy the trip! Our local expert will be on hand 24/7 while you're on the road.

PLAN AND BOOK YOUR TRIP AT
ROUGHGUIDES.COM/TRIPS

HOW TO DOWNLOAD YOUR FREE EBOOK

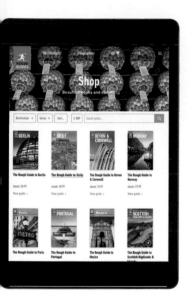

1. Visit **www.roughguides. com/free-ebook** or scan the **QR code** below

2. Enter the code **crete301**

3. Follow the simple step-by-step instructions

For troubleshooting contact: mail@roughguides.com

10 THINGS NOT TO MISS

Days 1–2

Iráklio. Pick up your hire car at Iráklio airport, check into a city hotel and look round the Archaeological Museum. Stroll through the old quarter, taking in the Historical and Religious Art museums in particular. Devote the following morning to Knossos Palace.

Days 2–3

Ágios Nikólaos and Spinalónga Island. After lunch in Iráklio, drive east to Ágios Nikólaos, choosing accommodation nearby and take in 'Ag Nik's' lakeside nightlife. The next morning, embark at Pláka for Spinalónga Island to visit the abandoned leper colony.

Days 3–4

Head east to Koureménos. Lunch in Ágios Nikólaos, then head east via Sitía to Moní Toploú and Vaï beach. Stay for two nights near Koureménos beach. On day 4, hike the Hohlahiés Gorge, and try windsurfing at Koureménos.

Day 5

Swim and overnight in Mýrtos. Proceed via Zíros and Makrý Gialós, stopping to swim at any of the beaches before lunch and a museum stop in Ierápetra. Continue west and overnight at peaceful Mýrtos.

Days 6–7

Rouvás Gorge. Drive inland from Mýrtos towards the Mesará valley, pausing at Áno Viánnos to take in its brilliantly frescoed church, before proceeding to Zarós for two nights. On day 7, walk the Rouvás Gorge or visit the monastic churches of Vrondísi and Ágios Fanoúrios. If any time remains, take the short detour to ancient Gortys.

OF **CRETE**

Day 8–9

Church visit. Continue west via the Minoan highlights of Phaistos and Agía Triáda. Stop for lunch at either Vóri or Mátala, and swim at the latter. Round off your day at Plakiás or Spíli, checking in for two nights. The next day involves an early start to tour the Amári Valley to visit its churches, with a possible late-afternoon swim at Ágios Pávlos beach.

Days 10–11

Sightseeing in Réthymno. Drive to Réthymno, stopping at Arkádi monastery en route, and stay in the atmospheric old town for two nights. Spend the next day taking in the old quarter, especially the massive Fortezza and the Historical and Folklore Museum.

Days 12–13

West towards Haniá. Proceed west towards Haniá, stopping for a swim and lunch at idyllic Lake Kourná. Arrive in Haniá for a two-night stay, choose a boutique hotel in the old quarter. The afternoon and next day can be spent savouring the old town's museums, shops and many restaurants.

Days 14–15

Hike Samariá Gorge. Park your car safely before taking an early bus up to the village of Xylóskala for the impressive descent of the Samariá Gorge. At the bottom, overnight at Agía Rouméli; then the following day, take a boat west to Soúgia or Paleóhora for another opportunity to swim. Finally, take a bus back to Haniá, retrieve your car, and drive to your departure airport.

CONTENTS

HIGHLIGHTS

A NOTE TO READERS

At Rough Guides, we always strive to bring you the most up-to-date information. This book was produced during a period of continuing uncertainty caused by the Covid-19 pandemic, so please note that content is more subject to change than usual. We recommend checking the latest restrictions and official guidance.

OVERVIEW

Crete: the name invokes a range of different images. Ancient sites to explore; commercial towns bustling with noise and traffic; millions of olive trees blanketing the countryside; raucous resorts with neon-lit bars and loud music; a romantic meal for two overlooking a small fishing port; mountains and gorges to trek through; a sunlounger on a beach, among hundreds of others, similarly soaking up the rays; 15 hours of sunshine a day in summer; three feet of snow in the mountains in winter. The island has something for everyone, and its sheer variety satisfies even the most jaded and cynical traveller.

THE 'GREAT ISLAND'

Crete is cast adrift in the eastern Mediterranean Sea, just 110 nautical miles north of the African coast and an even shorter sea-crossing from Anatolia. Its strategic position, at the crossroads of trade north from Egypt, west from Rome and east from the Middle East, made it valuable territory from the earliest days of trade and power politics.

Covering an area of 8,300 sq km (3,200 sq miles), Crete is sometimes called Megalónissos, or 'Great Island'. Visually, it is stunning, with three dramatic mountain ranges over 2,000m (6,500ft) high that seem to anchor the island in the sea. Water has cut vertiginous gorges through

Crete's provinces

Crete is divided into four administrative districts (*periféries* in Greek), mostly named after their governing cities: Iráklio, the most populous, with the island's capital; Haniá; Lasíthi (based in Ágios Nikólaos); and Réthymno.

the mountains and opened huge cave systems through their hearts. These caves were places of great religious significance to the ancient Cretans; in some cases, they were thought to be the birthplaces of Greek gods. Over the centuries, these caverns provided protection for pirates, vagabonds and freedom fighters. The mountains were never fully conquered, even during World War II – their furthest valleys were too remote, their slopes too steep. Today, their

Natural landscape

peaks are the domain of numerous birds of prey, including eagles, hawks and vultures.

Fertile plateaus and lowlands have been settled and farmed since Neolithic times; abundant fresh spring water from the surrounding peaks helped ensure a rich harvest. Around the coastline – especially in the north – long sandy stretches have attracted visitors since the 1960s, with the advent of package tours, but variety exists here too, with several different coastal environments; rocky coves, rugged headlands and marshy wetlands.

THE FRUITFUL YEAR

Despite its southerly latitude, seasons remain distinct on Crete. Springtime sees the hills awash with flowers and wheat crops ripening in the warming sun, goat kids are born and the flocks make the most of fresh pastures. As summer starts, cereals are harvested and the land takes on an ochre hue. Birdsong gives way to the sound of cicadas, and the smell of honeysuckle rises in the evening air. Midsummer sees Cretans seeking shade to escape the heat, while visitors head out in droves to work on their tans. The clanging of livestock bells can be heard across the countryside as flocks desperately search for sustenance in the parched hills.

Autumn brings a cooling of the temperature, yet a warming of the landscape as colours mellow in the lower arc of the late season sun. Stucco on buildings takes on a rosy hue, the grapes swell to tempting perfection and citrus fruits begin their transition from green to orange. All too soon, winter brings a blanket of snow to the mountains; ordinarily dry ravines and pastures swell with rain runoff, wood smoke fills the air, and folk retreat to their warm hearths.

The olive harvest is the main focal point of the year. This crop reigns supreme and millions of trees blanket hillside slopes and coastal plains, a symbol of man's reliance on the earth. It has sustained Cretans for far too long to be treated with disdain.

The inviting waters of the Gulf of Mirabéllo

THE CRADLE OF EUROPE

The footsteps of history can be seen on every dusty path and urban street. Crete was the cradle of European civilisation, and the Minoans – believed to be mythological until evidence of their existence was confirmed early in the 20th century – travelled far and wide across the eastern Mediterranean for trade. A prodigious collection of arte-facts now displayed in museums across the island shows them to be the first Indigenous European culture whose lives were graced by art, sports and the pursuit of pleasure. The Minoan civilisation suffered a sudden and terminal collapse around 1450BC for reasons that have not been established.

A devastating natural disaster was initially thought to be the cause, but archeological theories now consider either invasion by a warring people or internal revolt to be the most likely scenarios. Whatever the case, the catastrophe heralded the start of thousands of years of invasion and subjection for the Cretans: Mycenaeans, Dorians, Athenians, Macedonians, Romans, Byzantines, Arabs, Venetians and Ottomans all came to take control. Evidence of their presence abounds in the commanding fortresses, protective harbours, fine mansions, narrow winding alleys, elegant minarets and ornate fountains of the towns. In 1913, Crete finally achieved a long-awaited *énosis* (union) with Orthodox Christian Greece.

FREEDOM OR DEATH

Cretans did not take kindly to their native land being usurped and, particularly in the years of Turkish rule, they gained a reputation as formidable and tenacious fighters who struck with speed, then retreated to mountain strongholds to outwit their enemies.

They reverted back to the same lifestyle during World War II when Crete was captured by German forces, mounting a successful guerrilla resistance and living up to the old rallying cry – 'freedom or death'.

Invaders would occupy the cities, but they could never manage to tame the people of the countryside. For centuries, unbowed Cretans lived simple lives in harmony with the land; tending their flocks, growing fruit and vegetables, and harvesting the sea.

Clothes and carpets were made of wool, leather was used to make boots and saddles, wood was used for bowls and utensils, and grass and straw woven into basketry. Seasonal surpluses were stored to provide sustenance for the long winters that often isolated mountain villages. The people put their trust in God, as the many Orthodox churches across the island attest, praying for self-determination and for their menfolk hiding out in the hills.

ENDURING TRADITIONS

Although peace now reigns, a glance around communities in the Cretan heartland still suggests that little has changed. Whitewashed villages dot the landscape, each house with its own smallholding. The traditional diet – greens, olive oil, wild herbs, honey, yoghurt and a little lamb or goat meat – still sustains these rural people, and it has been scientifically proven to be one of the healthiest in the world. Though traditions are dying, some older men still stride out in black breeches, leather boots and crocheted headbands worn by previous generations while widows in black sit quietly knitting in their doorways and goats graze slopes that no farmer could use.

El Greco was born in Fódele

If a Cretan's hatred of his enemy is legendary, it has always been surpassed by generosity to his friends – and by extension to strangers (*xénos* is the Greek word for both stranger and friend). A door is always open to a passing traveller. Today, admiring an orchard or a ripening vineyard even in rudimentary Greek will often result in an armful of fruit to take with you on your journey – just a small example of how tradition carries on through the generations. And how do today's Cretans find their pleasure? Poetry, literature, music and dance; traditional forms of all these arts are still alive and well here.

Despite its traditions, Crete is also a very modern and urbanised island. Since the 1980s, many remote interior villages have all but emptied in favour of the largest coastal towns, expanding constantly. Young Cretans are just as interested in fashion, higher education and music as their peninsular-Greek cousins. They aim to find jobs with excitement, a secure future and ready cash to spend – something they feel a rural way of life cannot give them. Even in the ongoing economic downturn, the three largest north-coast towns of Iráklio, Réthymno and Haniá have active commercial sectors and vibrant intellectual scenes thanks to their universities and polytechnics, aspects of Crete that surprise many visitors.

Of course, the arrival of mass tourism has changed Crete, particularly along the northern coast where the majority of development has taken place. The island is invaded annually by an army of tourists who flock here in search of sunshine, relaxation and fun. Cretans seem happy to welcome everyone with precisely the kinds of activities that holidaymakers demand. However, there's luckily enough land area and individuality for Crete to ever be considered as just another 'Euro-island'. Fears of a cultural meltdown, while perhaps understandable, are wide off the mark. Gritty and enduring as ever, Cretans will continue to do things their way. This cultural distinction, its fascinating history and the dramatic landscape make Crete an enthralling holiday destination for decades to come.

HISTORY AND CULTURE

Crete's long history is bound up with its strategic position between Western Europe, the Middle East and North Africa. In good times, this brought trade, creative ideas and prosperity; in bad times, invasion, oppression and disease. Many fascinating legacies around the island attest to the complicated web that time has spun here.

The earliest human remains found on Crete date back to the seventh millennium BC. These first inhabitants were Neolithic hunter-gatherers who came from Asia Minor. They developed into farmers, with settlements and pastureland on the fertile Messará Plain. It was an influx of new, more skilled settlers shortly after 3000BC that ushered in the Minoan era, the first major civilisation to arise on European soil.

THE MINOANS

A great ancient Cretan civilisation was for many years believed to be merely the stuff of mythology. Yet with the discovery of cities and their marvellous artefacts, Sir Arthur Evans, its principal advocate, made reality out of folklore and myth (see page 41). We now know many facts about Minoan Crete – including that, at its zenith, the population of the island probably numbered more than two million, approximately four times greater than today's figure, with 100,000 people living in the capital, Knossos.

Bronze-Age Crete

Arthur Evans classified the three periods of Bronze-Age Crete as Early, Middle and Late Minoan, minutely subdivided. They are now known as the Pre-Palatial, Proto-Palatial, Neo-Palatial and Post-Palatial eras.

These early Bronze Age settlements were built without

A 3,500-year-old fresco of three Minoan women in Knossos

fortifications and comprised vast numbers of dwellings. The cities developed organically rather than to any grand design. The first palatial structures at Knossos, and other great cities such as Phaestos (modern Festós) and Malia, were erected between 2000–1900BC, but were all destroyed by an earthquake around 1700BC. The remains visible today are their replacements, even bigger and more splendid than the originals. This golden age of Minoan society – known as the Neo-Palatial era – lasted about 250 years.

Ruled by a priest-king, who presided over both religious and economic affairs, it is unclear whether one reigned over the entire island or if each palace settlement had its own regional king. His people worshipped the Mother Goddess, and divine power was symbolised by the bull, the focus of ornate and elaborate rituals. One sacred symbol, at odds with their peaceful lifestyle, is the *labrys* (double-headed axe). Its image has been found on various artefacts throughout the island.

The Minoans developed an alphabet and printing method, along with sophisticated plumbing and water-delivery systems. Women enjoyed high status, playing an active part in palace life, and the whole population enjoyed athletic contests, games and a whole range of recreational activities. Above all, they excelled in the visual arts.

Wherever there was a blank 'canvas', there was imagery: decorative entrances, walls, floors and pottery. Many breathtaking examples can be seen in the Archaeological Museum in Iráklio (see page 36). Even the smallest items, such as combs, were exquisitely crafted. Gold and precious stones were fashioned into beautiful jewellery, indicating a high quality of life, at least for certain classes of people.

What fuelled this great empire was trade. Cretans exhibited their skills not only with local resources such as paint, clay, copper and bronze, but also with imported raw materials – lapis lazuli from Afghanistan, ivory from Syria, gold, silver and black obsidian from Anatolia. Copper and bronze were worked and re-exported, along with high-value foodstuffs such as olive oil, honey and wine.

The Minoans developed into one of the great naval powers of the Mediterranean, with wood from the island's vast juniper and cypress forests providing material for boats. However, they concentrated their power more on commercial than military gain, showing a taste for the good life rather than a hunger for an empire.

This great civilisation came to a sudden, catastrophic end in around 1450BC. The exact cause remains unknown, but all the palaces were destroyed at the same time. Charred remains at Knossos and ash at Zakros suggest a great conflagration. A leading theory for many years was that natural disaster struck the island in the wake of the volcanic explosion on the island of Thíra (Santoríni), due north of Crete, bringing tidal waves, earthquakes and fire storms. But Thíra exploded in about 1500BC, a half-century before the Cretan destruction; more recent research has favoured another hypothesis – that an attack by invaders or domestic rebel forces may have brought about the end of this fine culture. Scholars will continue to debate the reason for many years to come.

DORIANS AND ROMANS

After the disaster, Mycenaean Greeks from the Peloponnese moved in

Lató was the dominant city during the Dorian occupation

to control what remained of the Minoan settlements – they may even have precipitated the destruction. Around 1200BC, Dorian invaders from the Balkans drove south through the Greek mainland, across the Aegean and into Crete.

Many coastal dwellers migrated to remote mountain settlements in order to escape their enemies. Others embarked on an overseas exodus that took them around the Mediterranean Sea. The island did not become directly involved in Greece's Persian and Peloponnesian Wars, although it became a valuable source of brave and energetic mercenaries.

While mainland Greece was reaching its zenith during the Classical Age (480–338BC), Crete remained a backwater of warring city-states, of which Gortys (modern Górtyna) was the most powerful. Nevertheless, enlightened Athenians acknowledged Crete as a source of much of their culture, and its caves and shrines were major centres of pilgrimage. The island's most

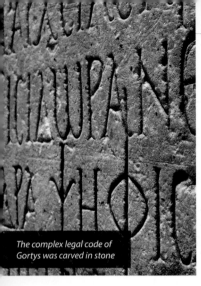

The complex legal code of Gortys was carved in stone

important achievement – and only significant remnant – from this period is the law code of Gortys (see page 45). It reveals a hierarchical society of free men, serfs and the enslaved ruled by an aristocratic class. It took the Romans three years of brutal fighting to conquer Crete in 67BC, and they did so only by playing the rival city-states against one another. Crete remained a province of the Roman Empire until AD395, with Gortys as its capital. The Romans brought a certain order to the island, putting an end to internal struggles, building new roads, ports and aqueducts, and introducing systems of domestic plumbing and central heating not much worse than those found today.

EARLY CHRISTIANS

The apostle Paul arrived in AD60–61, and by AD64 had charged his disciple Titus to convert the islanders to Christianity. Titus had a hard time combating local pagan beliefs, but died peacefully in AD107, as bishop of Gortys, and Titus (Ágios Títos in Greek) became Crete's patron saint.

When Roman power split in two, the eastern Byzantine Empire inherited the island (though its hold on islands in the south Aegean were, in reality, nominal). Attacks by pirates and Islamic forces brought terror to the people, but Cretans remained loyal to the Orthodox Church throughout the occupation, by Andalucian pirates, of AD824–961. The island was recaptured after a terrible siege of Iráklio by Byzantine commander (and subsequently emperor) Nikeforos Phokas, during which he catapulted the heads of dead Arabs into the city to dishearten surviving defenders.

VENETIAN DAYS

After Byzantium fell to the Crusaders in 1204, Crete was given to their leader, Boniface of Montferrat, who immediately sold it to Venice for 1,000 silver marks, ushering in a new era. Crete prospered greatly under the 465 years of Venetian occupation (1204–1669), although during the first century, there were repeated revolts by both Venetian colonists and displaced Byzantine aristocracy. As a source of shipbuilding timber in a key location, the island was a linchpin in the far-flung commercial empire, and became the Republic's first formally constituted overseas colony.

Proudly emblazoned with the Lion of St Mark, the ports and fortifications of Iráklio (called Candia under Venetian rule, as was the whole of Crete), Haniá and Réthymno bear witness to the Venetians' ambitious public building programme. Several villas and loggias still attest to their style of living. After the 14th century, upper-class Cretans began to intermarry with the occupiers and to participate in their style of government.

The arts flourished during the 15th and 16th centuries, a period known as the Cretan Renaissance. Numerous new

The Church's role

The Greek Orthodox Church has always played a special role on Crete. Under foreign domination, the Church funded and organised schools where Greek language and traditions were taught and kept alive. Most significantly, it was the focus of unity and resistance to oppression, as indicated by the many attacks on Crete's 34 monasteries.

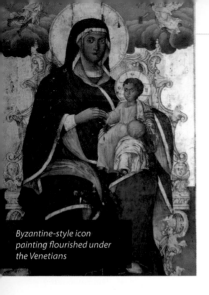

Byzantine-style icon painting flourished under the Venetians

monasteries and churches were built. Icon-painting attained new heights after an influx of artists from around Byzantium after 1453, who founded important schools of art.

The great literary figure of the time, Vitsentzos Kornaros (1553–1613), wrote a romantic epic poem in Cretan dialect, the *Erotokritos*. Even if most villagers can no longer recite it by heart, it is still acclaimed among the literati of Crete.

THE BATTLE FOR CRETE

In the eastern Mediterranean, Christian forces were in retreat as a new Muslim power began to expand. The Ottoman Turks pushed Venetian and Genoese forces out of Asia Minor and the Greek mainland, and then from most islands of the Aegean. Eventually, it would be Crete's turn. The Ottomans waged a titanic war to wrest the island from the Venetians. It began with raids on Haniá, Réthymno and Sitía in the 1530s by the notorious pirate-admiral Hayreddin Barbarossa. Over the next century, the Venetians greatly strengthened the fortifications, but Haniá and Réthymno fell anyway in 1645.

Two years later, the Turks laid siege to the capital, Candia. It was an epic struggle, which was to last 22 years. Initially weakened by an outbreak of plague, the 12,000-strong population rallied to the defence. After 15 years, the Turkish commander, Hüseyin Pasha, was summoned back to Constantinople and publicly strangled for his failure to take the city. Supposedly 30,000 defenders died, but there were 118,000 fatalities among the besiegers.

Although Western Europe's leaders watched with bated breath, they sent little support, and inexorably Venetian resistance was worn down. As the conquerors entered the city gates in 1699, the Venetians negotiated an orderly departure, taking with them, among other Christian artefacts, the head of St Titus. This most cherished of Crete's religious relics was not to return to the island until 1966.

OTTOMAN RULE

Crete's years spent under the Ottomans (1669–1898) largely constituted a period of cultural and economic stagnation. Imperial

THE CRETAN RENAISSANCE

After the fall of Constantinople in 1453, Crete became a haven for artists and theologians fleeing the Ottomans. A religious college for the study of painting, theology and the humanities was established at the Church of Agía Ekateríni in Iráklio (see page 36), which became the centre of the Cretan Renaissance during the 16th and 17th centuries. El Greco is said to have studied here, along with his contemporary Mihaïl Damaskinos, and Vitsentzos Kornaros, the author of the epic poem *Erotokritos*.

Cretan artists excelled at icon painting, blending traditional Byzantine style with influences from Renaissance Italy. Their work was in demand throughout the Western world. Damaskinos, who worked in Venice from 1577 to 1582, was the master of this art. His use of colour and perspective brought a depth to the icon tradition that was widely imitated.

leaders had no interest in developing or investing in this new domain and, after the occasionally oppressive but at times brilliant centuries of Venetian government, Crete slid back into a dark age.

Apart from repairing the islands' fortifications, the Ottomans left relatively few lasting remnants of their rule. They built few mosques – largely because many Cretan converts adhered to the heterodox Bektaşi sect – and left only a few houses in the largest towns, where they made up nearly half of the population until the 1840s. Most numerous of their legacies are the ornate street fountains found in the corners of market squares and outside chapels. Throughout this period, many town-dwelling Cretans kept a low profile. They publicly converted to Islam to escape taxes, continuing to practise their Orthodox faith in secret.

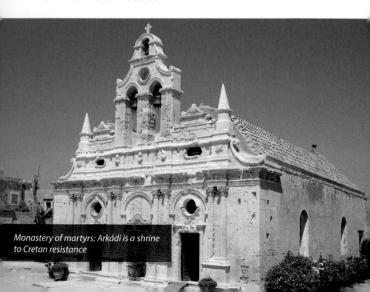

Monastery of martyrs: Arkádi is a shrine to Cretan resistance

There were sporadic attempts at revolt, which were often launched from remote mountain strongholds where rebels could survive in safety. The more vulnerable communities on the lower plains paid a high price for these violent revolts in the form of swift and bloody reprisals.

National day

Crete celebrates its National Day on 8 November, the anniversary of the explosion in 1866 at Arkádi Monastery, where hundreds of Cretan rebels died rather than surrender to the Turks.

The first major rebellion occurred in 1770 when the Russians, hoping to distract the Turks while they waged their own attacks on the Ottoman Empire elsewhere, promised aid to Daskalogiannis, a wealthy shipowner. He raised a revolt in Sfakiá, but the support never arrived. The rebellion was crushed, Daskalogiannis was flayed alive, and the whole sorry event became the subject of a rousing epic poem.

However, once part of Greece had achieved independence from the Ottoman Empire after 1830, the atmosphere changed. After two decades of rule by an Egyptian vassal of the sultan, various forms of semi-autonomous rule, with representation for Christian notables, were attempted, but to no avail. Insurgencies recurred, generally put down with considerable severity; for the Cretan resisters, death came to form a monumental collective badge of honour.

During the major 1866 uprising, hundreds of Christian Cretans – and many Muslims – died in a suicide explosion at Arkádi Monastery. There were more insurgencies in 1889 and 1895. The island's repeated suffering was duly celebrated in the popular, heroic *Songs of Digenis* (adapted from their medieval origins for the modern struggle), Pandelis Prevelakis' particularly grim novel *The Cretan*, and the lofty writings of Níkos Kazantzákis.

UNION WITH GREECE

Finally, in 1898, the European powers forced the Ottomans to grant Crete autonomy within the empire and accept Prince George, second son of King George of Greece, as high commissioner. This did not satisfy Cretan nationalists, and the prince, presiding over an island divided into ultra-nationalist and accommodationist parliamentary factions, resigned in 1906. It was only in 1913, under the leadership of the Cretan Eleftherios Venizelos, that *énosis* (union) with Greece was achieved.

Despite being unscathed by World War I, Crete saw major changes between 1913 and the mid-1920s. Muslim Cretans had been leaving for Rhodes, the Middle East and Anatolia since 1897, but the disastrous 1919–22 Greek invasion of Turkey, and the ultimately successful Turkish resistance to it, greatly accelerated this movement through the compulsory population exchange between Greece and Turkey in 1923. The last of thousands of Muslims were expelled, with Orthodox refugees from Asia Minor arriving to take their place.

WAR AND PEACE

Yet Crete's travails were not yet over. During World War II, the rapid advance of the German forces through mainland Greece in 1941 forced the Allies to retreat to Crete. On 20 May, German paratroopers secured the airfield at Máleme, just west of Haniá. British, Australian and New Zealand soldiers joined Cretan militia during a valiant defence in the ten-day Battle of Crete, but were ultimately forced to retreat across the island. Many were evacuated to Egypt, though several thousand were left stranded and fled to safety in the mountains.

Casualties on both sides were terrible and numerous: Allied losses numbered 2,000 killed and 12,000 taken prisoner, while the German war cemetery contains almost 4,500 graves.

With their tradition of opposition to foreign invaders, Cretans immediately began resistance activities against the occupying German force. Initial efforts to shelter stranded Allied servicemen and smuggle them off the island in small groups from isolated south-coast beaches were remarkably successful. But after the Italian capitulation in September 1943, brutal German reprisals against civilians became more frequent. In early 1944, the resistance pulled off an amazing coup by kidnapping the German commander, General Kreipe, and smuggling him off the island. Subsequently, German forces burnt many villages and killed many men of fighting age in the Amári Valley. The occupation of Crete did not completely end until May 1945, when the Germans abandoned Haniá. Many Cretan towns were left in tattered ruins from heavy bombing, but Crete largely escaped the internal strife of the civil war that raged in mainland Greece (1946–49) and felt fewer effects of the oppressive colonels' junta (1967–74) than many other Greek communities.

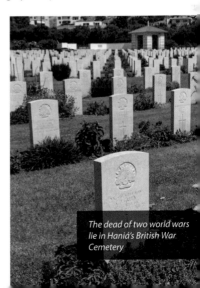

In 1981, Greece became a full member of the European Community, and Andreas Papandreou's PASOK party, with overwhelming support from Crete (who saw it as heir to the Venizelist tradition), won elections to form Greece's first quasi-socialist government. Papandreou's son, George, became prime minister in 2009, presiding

The dead of two world wars lie in Haniá's British War Cemetery

over economic collapse and charged by Greece's creditors with essentially undoing most of his father's legacy, before being replaced by a technocratic unity coalition in 2011. In 2012, the leader of New Democracy Antonis Samaras became prime minister, and the country started pursuing further austerity measures. However, in 2014, the Greek unemployment rate rose to a record high of 28 percent.

In 2015, the Greeks turned from right-wing New Democracy to left-wing SYRIZA and chose its leader, Alexis Tsipras, as the new prime minister. Soon after holding a national referendum in the same year, Tsipras signed the Third bailout agreement, according to which Greece would be given a loan of around 84 billion euros. In return, the country would have to introduce a number of reforms, including increasing VAT and privatizing a number of state assets. However, a group of MPs from SYRIZA heavily opposed these controversial reforms and stirred a rebellion inside the party. Consequently, after five months, Tsipras stepped down from office, only to return a month later. During his short absence, Vassiliki Thanou-Christophilou took over his duties, becoming the first female prime minister in Greece. In 2017, general and youth unemployment rates held at 22 and 44 percent, respectively.

Faced with mounting disillusionment with further bailout terms and increased taxes, SYRIZA's luck finally ran out when New Democracy were returned to power with almost 40 percent of the vote in the 2019 elections. Prime Minister Kyriakos Mistotakis introduced a raft of typical right-wing measures such as restrictions on the right to strike, but was praised for his government's initial handling of the 2020 global Covid-19 pandemic by imposing tough restrictions early on. The country was even able to open up for a short tourist season in 2020 and a longer one in 2021, although visitor numbers remained well below the annual average, meaning that economic recovery remains a distant dream.

HISTORICAL LANDMARKS

c. **6500–2600BC** Settlers arrive in Crete from Asia Minor.

2600–2000BC Pre-Palatial era: immigrants bring copper and pottery.

2000–1700BC Proto-Palatial period: discovery of bronze; language written down; first palaces built, then destroyed by earthquake.

1700–1450BC Neo-Palatial era: the golden age of Minoan civilisation.

c.**1450BC** Minoan palaces destroyed; Mycenaeans arrive.

c.**1150BC** Dorians from northern Greece conquer most of Crete.

67BC Crete becomes a Roman province, with Gortys the capital.

395 Roman Empire splits permanently, Crete allotted to Byzantium.

824–961 Arabs conquer Crete, destroy Gortys, make their capital at fortress of Rabdh el-Khandak (Iráklio).

961 Nikephoros Fokas recaptures Crete for Byzantium.

1204 Venetians acquire Crete, rule for 465 years from Candia (Iráklio).

1669 Turks capture Candia after 22-year siege and control all Crete.

1821–7 Greek War of Independence; Crete under Egyptian control.

1898 European Great Powers occupy Crete, which becomes an autonomous principality within the Ottoman Empire.

1913 Crete finally becomes part of Greece.

1923 Last Muslims expelled from Crete; Christians arrive from Asia Minor.

1941–5 Germany occupies Crete: heavy losses, villages destroyed.

1971 Iráklio replaces Haniá as capital of Crete.

1981 Greece joins the European Union. First socialist government.

2002 The euro becomes the currency of Greece.

2004 Greece hosts the Olympics in Athens.

2010–11 Greece effectively bankrupt, dependent on IMF/EU loans.

2014 Greek unemployment rises to a record high of 28 percent.

2015 The Greeks consent to the Third bailout agreement.

2015 Vassiliki Thanou-Christophilou becomes the first female prime minister in Greece.

2019 New Democracy return to power amidst continuing austerity.

2020–22 Covid-19 hits Greece, and the harsh lockdown measures imposed save it from the high cases and deaths seen elsewhere in Europe.

Haniá's Venetian harbour

OUT AND ABOUT

Crete is a big island – within the five largest in the Mediterranean – so if you want to see lots of what it has to offer, choose your itinerary carefully. Staying at a central base allows for excursions to both the east and west, whereas a base in the far east or west limits your ability to see the opposite end of the island easily.

This guide divides Crete into four sections: the capital, Iráklio, followed by the central section; then moving east, before finally exploring the western parts of the island. The major attractions are covered, so that you can plan your itinerary around them, but remember that the countryside is filled with hidden treasures; traditional communities, frescoed churches and mountain paths, all waiting to be discovered.

IRÁKLIO

Iráklio ❶ comes as a surprise to travellers used to Greek island ports further north in the Aegean Sea. It is the fourth-largest Greek city (population approximately 160,000), and the commercial and administrative heart of Crete. Despite current hard times – winter unemployment exceeds 25 percent – there is a lively scene based around its university, and a sophistication to match other medium-sized mainland Greek university towns, such as Pátra or Ioánnina. However, this is not the only facet of the city. Around the harbour you'll still find a fishing industry based on small family-owned boats, and in the narrow backstreets a few surviving small workshops.

Truth be told, Iráklio is far from an attractive town; heavy bombing during World War II was compounded by thoughtless postwar development, and only recently have its crumbling

The Venetian fortress guards the harbour at Iráklio

medieval quarters, public monuments and surviving older build-ings received the preservation attention they deserve. Yet be sure to take time to explore the narrow lanes beyond the traffic-clogged main boulevards, and you will be rewarded.

Iráklio was a thriving port in Minoan times and became known as Heracleum under Roman rule. The Andalusians, who established the Emirate of Crete, built a huge castle here while the Venetians chose it as their capital, giving the name Candia to both the city and the whole island. Candia prospered from Venetian trade and when Turkish forces stormed the island, the town held out for 22 years before falling in 1669. As Kandiye, it became a relative back-water of the Ottoman Empire, only to rise to prominence again following union with Greece. It was declared capital again in 1971, taking the title from Haniá in the west. It is also worth mention-ing that Iráklio is the birthplace of the painter El Greco, whose real name was Doménikos Theotokópoulos.

THE CITY CENTRE

The city centre lies within the vast fortress started by the Venetians and reinforced by the Ottomans. One can walk along sections of its walls to gain an impression of how large the citadel once was. The heart of Iráklio is the small **Platía Venizélou** (Venizelos Square), with its fringe of cafés and restaurants. At its centre, the **Morosini Fountain** Ⓐ dates from Venetian times, though its sombre lion statues are 300 years older and lend the widely used nickname of Platía Leondária (Lions' Square). From here, most of Iráklio's attractions are only a few minutes' walk – the closest, which flanks the plaza, being **Ágios Márkos** (St Mark's), a Venetian church, now the municipal art gallery.

North along the pedestrianised Ikostipémptis Avgoústou (25th August Street) looms the impressive façade of the **Venetian Loggia**, originally dating from 1628 but reconstructed after World War II. Iráklio's municipal offices divide themselves between here and the adjacent Andrógeio Mégaro. Walk around the loggia to find the **Church of Ágios Títos** Ⓑ. Founded late in the first millennium, it honours St Titus, the island's first bishop and patron saint. When the church was consecrated, Titus's body was brought here from Gortys and re-interred. The Venetians took his remains to Venice when they fled the

What's in a name?

Iráklio was first named Heracleum by the Romans, before the Andalucian Arabs changed its name to Rabdh-al-Khandaq – becoming Hándax for the Greeks under Nikephoros Phokas who soon re-conquered it. The Venetians renamed it Candia. During the Ottoman occupation, Muslims knew it as Kandiye, while the Cretans called it Megalo Kastro (Big Fortress), until the name Iráklio was officially adopted in 1913.

island and the church was rebuilt as the Vezir Mosque after an 1856 earthquake, resulting in the incongruous but beautiful decoration on the outer walls. In 1966 the Venetian authorities returned the skull of St Titus to Ágios Títos in a gold reliquary, along with fine paintings depicting scenes of the saint's life. Just west lies a small park supplied with more cafés.

THE HARBOUR AREA

Continuing down 25th August Street leads to the waterfront and the majestic **Koulés** Venetian fortress Ⓒ (http://koules.efah.gr; Wed–Mon: mid-June to Aug 8am–8pm; Sep 8am–7pm; Oct 8am–6pm; Nov–March 8.30am–3.30pm; April to mid-June 8.30am–4.30pm) out on the breakwater, built to protect the old harbour. En route you'll pass vaulted remains of the large, arcaded **arsenália** (repair depots) that serviced Venetian ships, and the city's fishing fleet – small colourful boats with piles of yellow nets. The fortress was completed in 1540 to protect the town against the Ottoman threat and, with the circuit of walls inland, explains how Candia held out long after the rest of Crete had fallen. The fortress was reopened in 2016 with a completely new exhibition presenting the history of the edifice. A tour of the interior reveals a strong and efficient design; there are wonderful views from its ramparts.

A short walk west along the waterfront, past the disused Dominican monastery of Ágios Pétros (St Peter), brings you to the **Historical Museum of Crete** Ⓓ (www.historical-museum.gr; April–Oct Mon–Fri (except Tues) 10am–5pm, Sat & Sun 11am–5pm; Nov–March Mon–Fri 9am–3.30pm, Sat 10am–4pm), housed in an impressive building that is part Venetian mansion, part modern glass edifice. The museum – thematically rather than chronologically – covers Cretan history from the Byzantine Empire to the present, as well as ethnography. There are exquisite icons and fresco fragments rescued from churches across the island, stone relief carvings, documentation of the local Jewish, Muslim and Armenian communities, folk textiles and a re-creation of a traditional Cretan home. Models and prints of Iráklio across the centuries show how the townscape has developed, as does an interactive model of the medieval city, showing the many monuments sadly destroyed since 1897. Due prominence is given to the struggle for Cretan independence and World War II resistance (including the 1942 sabotage of the local German airfield), as well as the only two, small El Greco paintings still on Crete.

The **Natural History Museum of Crete** ⓔ (www.nhmc.uoc.gr; Mon–Fri 9am–5pm, Sat & Sun 10am–6pm) lies just west, housed in a former seafront power plant. The museum has interesting displays of flora and fauna as well as an earthquake simulator, where visitors can experience an earthquake of magnitude up to 6 degrees on the Richter scale (there are sessions every half hour).

SOUTH OF THE CITY CENTRE

South of Lions' Square is **1866 Street**, nicknamed 'Market Street', which still retains some of the atmosphere of an old bazaar. Here you can stroll past stalls selling fresh produce and souvenirs, or eat at the numerous *ouzeris* that serve the market workers. At the southern end of Market Street is **Platía Kornárou** ⓕ (Kornárou Square) where you will find

The market on 1866 Street

a hexagonal Ottoman pumphouse (now a café) beside the **Bembo Fountain** (Kríni Bémbou), created in 1588 using numerous pieces of architectural spolia, including the torso of a Roman statue.

A short walk northwest from here along the inner arterial road brings you to **Platía Agías Ekaterínis** (St Catherine's Square) where the 19th-century cathedral of Ágios Minás dwarfs two older religious buildings. The small church immediately adjacent is also called **Ágios Minás**, with a splendidly ornate iconostasis – if the church is closed, ask in the cathedral for the key. Behind these two churches is the 15th-century shrine that gives the square its name: **Agía Ekateríni** (St Catherine). It originally belonged to St Catherine's monastery in the Egyptian Sinai, and served as a monastic school. Today it houses the **St Catherine's Museum** 🅖 (http://iakm.gr/agia; Mon–Sat 9.30am–7.30pm, Sun 10.30am–7.30pm) with a wealth of art from churches and monasteries across the island, including six large icons by the celebrated Cretan artist Mihaïl Damaskinos.

THE ARCHAEOLOGICAL MUSEUM

Walk southeast from Lions' Square along the pedestrianised shopping street, Dedálou, to reach the city's top attraction, the **Archaeological Museum of Iráklio** 🅗 (www.heraklionmuseum. gr; April–Oct daily 8am–5pm; Nov Mon & Wed–Sun 8am–5pm, Tues 10am–5pm; Dec–March Mon & Wed–Sun 8.30am–3.30pm, Tues 10am–5pm). One of the greatest archeological collections in the world, this brings together finds from sites across Crete and from every era of the island's ancient history. Pride of place goes to the best Minoan artefacts.

As the pre-eminent centre of this ancient people, Crete is the main source of information and excavated remains concerning the Minoans. For any other museum this would be treasure enough, yet there are also impressive Greek and Roman artefacts to enjoy. The extensively renovated museum is a must for those intending to visit the ancient sites, since the objects here add life to the now-empty cities and palaces. To fully appreciate its glories will take several hours – the exquisite detail on pottery and frescoes, and the fine workmanship in jewellery and every-day tools is breathtaking. Try to visit in the early morning or late afternoon to avoid the large tour groups who arrive at around midday. The 24 rooms are arranged in chronological order from the Neolithic to the Roman period, grouping artefacts from each site; only a room devoted to Minoan wall-paintings and sculptures breaks this chronological arrangement. Below are some of the highlights of your tour.

The earliest finds are from 7000BC (Neolithic and Pre-Palatial periods). Many were found at Móhlos on the northeastern coast.

Primitive pottery is on dis-play – including a rather naive clay bull with an acro-bat holding one horn – and finer work such as a stone *pyxis* (jewellery box) incised with geometric patterns and a reclining animal.

Finds from the Proto-Palatial period (2000–1700BC) include the earliest examples of fine Kamáres ware pottery, found in the ruins at Knossos. Fascinating miniature work is also in evi-dence, with a series of tiny faience plaques depicting the façades of Minoan houses.

Ornamental artefact in the Archaeological Museum

Public outcry

In 1979 Prime Minister Constantine Karamalís wanted to loan part of the Minoan collection abroad. The Cretans took to the streets armed, protesting against the removal of their historical art treasures from the Iráklio Archaeological Museum.

The finest find uncovered at the Phaistos Palace is **Phaistos Disc**, a clay disc 16cm (6.25in) in diameter, imprinted with hieroglyphic and geometric symbols that have yet to be deciphered.

Finds from the golden age of Minoan society – the Neo-Palatial period (1700–1450BC) – include artefacts originated in the palaces of Knossos, Mália and Phaistos. It is worth mentioning the superb *rhyton* (libation vessel) carved from black steatite in the shape of a bull's head. The bull was one of the foremost religious symbols of the Minoans and this piece was created by one of the pre-eminent artisans of the time.

There are also objects from the final phase of Minoan civilisation (1450–1400BC). The pottery and stonework is worth studying, but the chief artefacts are the Linear A script fragments incised on thin clay plates and not yet deciphered. Also exhibited are examples of Linear B, which was deciphered in 1952 and is of Mycenaean origin – showing that by the time the tablet was written the Minoans had lost control of the major cities.

Also on display here is a delightful clay model of a Minoan dwelling, complete with roof terrace and tiny windows to keep out the bright sun and fierce Cretan winds.

Tomb finds that date from the Neo-Palatial and Post-Palatial periods include beautiful pottery pieces, military artefacts such as helmets and sword handles, and splendid gold jewellery.

The collection of domestic utensils and personal objects found in the palaces and around the *Megara* (royal chambers) includes stone vessels, pottery, hammers and a potter's wheel. There are several intricately carved steatite vessels, including the **Harvester Vase** discovered at Agía Triáda and decorated with a low relief of men at work in the fields.

A number of items come from the palace of Zakros in the far east of Crete. The 'marine' amphora is decorated with octopuses and Argonauts. A delicate rock-crystal *rhyton* shows the sophistication of both workmanship and personal taste in the Neo-Palatial period. There are finds from other sites in eastern Crete, artefacts from the Post-Palatial period (1400–1100BC), and the period between 1100BC and 650BC, including a large collection of gold jewellery. A number of painted Minoan sarcophagi, many decorated with the images of fish or birds are displayed.

The Archaeological Museum of Iráklio is the place to see the finest surviving **frescoes** found throughout the Minoan kingdoms, dating from 1600 to 1400. They depict the enigmatic Minoans at work and play, and their major influences – the bull, other animals and the marine environment. Male figures – presumably out in the sun more – were always rust coloured, while more secluded females were always painted white.

The spiral decoration of the only stone **sarcophagus** found on the island (at Agía Triáda) frames scenes of libation and other religious activities. You can also examine a miniature re-creation of

The famous 'bull-leaping' fresco shows a daring acrobatic game

The Agía Triáda sarcophagus shows tributes imported from Africa

the palace of Knossos, completed according to early hypotheses on its design.

The **Ring of King Minos** is an engraved Minoan gold ring found in 1928 close to the Knossos palace, and long considered to be a hoax before being verified by experts in 2002.

The museum has a shop, which sells books and postcards, a café and there are several more just across the street from the entrance. Also opposite is the busy main tourist office (Mon–Fri 9am–3pm).

A treat for contemporary art-lovers is the Museum of Visual Arts (https://metheraklion-gr; Mon–Fri 6–8.30pm), located at Nymphon 3, further east from the Archaeological Museum. Established in 2000, it exhibits works from the finest contemporary artists of Cretan descent.

CENTRAL CRETE

Central Crete is the market garden and vineyard of the island, with fertile valleys nestling between rocky mountain ranges. Today it supplies much of the fresh produce for the population, including grapes for the quaffable Cretan country wine. This is not a recent development: it was home to the Minoans, with their most famous palace only a few kilometres away from Iráklio. The Roman capital was also located in this region. Around these important archeological sites are farming communities quite different in character from the city and the coastal resorts. Spend time exploring these villages for a glimpse of a lifestyle that will soon disappear as the younger generation forsakes rural ways of life.

KNOSSOS

Just 5km (3 miles) south of Iráklio is **Knossos** ❷ (daily: winter 8.30am–5pm; summer 8am–6pm), now famed worldwide as the place where Sir Arthur Evans (at that time Director of the Ashmolean Museum in Oxford) found proof that the mythical ancient civilisation of Crete had really existed. Evans named this people the Minoans after their most-famous, semi-mythical king – Minos. He began digging in 1900 after buying the site, financing the excavation programme with his own money, and almost immediately struck the first masonry of a huge Bronze Age palace replete with magnificent pottery and other artefacts.

Evans' subsequent attempts to reconstruct areas of the palace have met with intense criticism from other scholars but Knossos (Knossós in modern Greek) is now Crete's premier attraction, and rightly so. Although there is no documented proof, the majority of Cretans believe that Knossos was the site of the famed battle between Theseus and the Minotaur in the Labryinth below King Minos's palace.

The first palace at Knossos was built c.2000BC in the Proto-Palatial era, but this was destroyed by a massive earthquake only 300 years later. Most of what you see here today are the remains of the second palace, built following the disaster. This coincided with a golden age of Minoan society (the Neo-Palatial era, from 1700BC), when the people grew rich through trade and artistic endeavour was at its peak. The palace expanded continuously through the following years, resulting in a complex of around 1,200 small rooms several storeys high covering over 20,000 sq m (215,280 sq ft). This golden era came to an end in 1450BC, and major fire caused catastrophic damage around 1350BC, but although the palace was completely destroyed, the surrounding town continued to be occupied until the 5th century AD.

The palace was erected around a large **Central Court**, possibly used for public meetings, which now forms the heart of the site. Imagine Minoans at play here as depicted on the pottery and frescoes in the Archaeological Museum in Iráklio – acrobats and dancers as well as the famed bull-leapers. Visitors enter past what remains of the **West Court**, used as an entryway to a **West Wing**, where the administrative and religious activities took place. Minoans would walk down the corridor of processions past frescoed walls to reach the **propylaia** (sacred entranceway). A **grand staircase** then led north to the most important official chambers within this wing, its sturdy painted colonnades typical of those found throughout the palace.

The lower floor here houses the **throne room**, with ornate griffin frescoes and a lustral basin for ritual purification. The walls – lined with stone seats thought to have been used by advisers or councillors – would have been decorated with red plaster and an ornamental dado. In the northeastern corner was a crypt where a cache

MINOAN BUILDING METHODS

Knossos construction methods were complicated, with light wells illuminating lower chambers, and polythyra, masonry supports to create structural integrity, between which were large wooden doors serving as partitions. Cypress or juniper trunks served as anti-seismic cushioning in walls, and the same wood (often poised upside down) used as columns. Many quarters were semi-subterranean for more comfort in the warm climate, with high windows for ventilation.

of treasures was unearthed during the excavations.

A staircase by the throne room leads to what Evans christened the **piano nobile** – a reconstructed upper floor of the west wing. Next to the staircase is the **Tripartite Shrine** where the Linear B alphabetical tablets were discovered.

On the east side of the court, a **grand staircase** leads to the royal chambers or *Megara*, where some of the best-preserved rooms

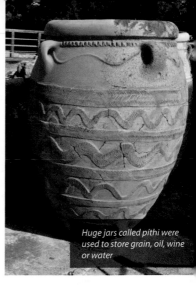

Huge jars called píthi were used to store grain, oil, wine or water

can be found. The shallow gypsum staircase is a stunning construction and one of the masterpieces of Minoan architecture. Notice the clever use of lighting wells to illuminate the lowest storeys (there were four in total). The **King's Megaron** is decorated with a simple wooden throne, although the antechamber walls are incised with images of the double axe or *labrys*, so important to the mythology surrounding Knossos. The room is also known as the **Hall of the Double Axes**. The architecture of this room is typically Neo-Palatial in style, with large *polythyra* supporting the roof. It is thought that large wooden doors were fitted between the pillars and that these could be removed to create a *stoa* (open-fronted arcade), if the king wished it. The **Queen's Megaron** has a splendid dolphin fresco lining one wall. On the far side of the site are the remains of the Royal Road leading north to the coast, still in exceptional condition.

Evans made numerous remarkable finds at the site, since it had been covered and left undisturbed following the 1350BC disaster.

Pottery intricately painted with marine life, bronze figurines and exquisite jewels – many of these were discovered in the rock-cut tombs of the Post-Palatial period. Yet it is the mundane and simple things that make Knossos so utterly fascinating. Evidence of early water piping, central heating and sanitation systems show a remarkable sophistication.

TOWARDS GORTYS (GÓRTYNA)

Other classical sites lay below Iráklio near the south coast. The **Nikos Kazantzakis Museum** (Myrtia; www.kazantzaki.gr; April–Oct daily 9am–5pm; Nov–March Mon–Fri & Sun 10am–3pm) is located around 6km (4 miles) south of Knossos. The museum exhibits the intellectual heritage of one of the most acknowledged Cretan author and philosopher, Nikos Kazantzakis.

Take the road southwest to **Agía Varvára**, in a vine-filled valley skirting the looming Psilorítis range to the west. Beyond lies the

RITES AND SACRIFICES

In the Minoan civilisation, the bull symbolised virility and all natural forces. The walls of the palace of Knossos are covered in paintings and sculptures of huge sacred horns. In the courtyard, young people used to perform an acrobatic game where they had to grab the bull's horns and leap above the animal. Every year, a bull was caught, its throat slit and its blood collected. This sacrifice bound Minoan society and the animal's divine powers to the great cycles of nature. The Mother Goddess was represented by the Snake Goddess's bare breasts, a symbol of fertility. The snake itself was a symbol of reincarnation and healing. The sacred pillar embodied the goddess, while the double-headed axe represented the moon and the double power – religious and political – of the priest-king.

The remains of the 6th-century Basilica of Ágios Títos at Gortys

Mesará Plain, a wide fertile valley surrounded by hills and a centre for farming since ancient times. For a pretty drive through the foothills on the north, take the direct road to **Zarós ❸** from Agía Varvára. The scenery is magnificent, with plenty to do locally: idle by the **Votamós lake**, hike the **Rouvás Gorge** just north, or visit the small, frescoed **Moní Vrondisíou** (Vrondísi Monastery) 4km (2.5 miles) away on the **Kamáres** road; this was the original home of the Damaskinos icons, now in Agía Ekateríni in Iráklio.

A little bit further, at Vorízia, is the turning for **Ágios Fanoúrios** (Varsamónero; June–Oct Mon–Sat 8.30am–3pm), another monastic church with vivid 15th-century frescoes. Beyond Kamáres, with its famous cave overhead, the same road continues towards the Amári Valley to the west (see page 73).

To reach the ancient sites drop directly down from Agía Varvára to the Mesará. Near **Ágii Déka** – named after ten saints who were martyred here, and whose purported catacomb is still viewable at the village's west edge – are the ancient remains of **Gortys ❹** (Górtyna), capital of the island during the Roman era (from 67BC) but already an important city in Minoan times.

Gortys is such a huge site – at its height it had a population of 300,000 – that you will see signposts to remains lying amidst olive groves, south of the modern road. By following the signage, you will be rewarded with ancient columns resting against olive trees, shards of pottery among the grass, and a governor's palace and amphitheatre to explore.

The fenced main site (daily: summer 8am–8pm; winter 8.30am–3pm) covers only a tiny part of the city, but it protects one of the most important archeological finds on Crete – the **Law Code** dating from the Dorian period, around 500BC. This huge stone tablet was incised with script setting forth the rules on marriage, criminal justice, property and inheritance rights. The tablet is incorporated into the rear of a small Roman **odeion**. The site entrance is dominated by the triple apse of the 6th-century **Basilica of Ágios Títos** (St Titus), all that remains after Arab raiders razed most of the building in AD 825.

PHAISTOS

Travel on through the village of Mires to reach **Phaistos** ❺ (Festós), the site of an impressive Minoan palace (daily: summer 8am–8pm; winter 8.30am–5pm). As Gortys rose in prominence towards the end of the first millennium BC, the fortunes of Phaistos declined,

KAMÁRES POTTERY

Kamáres vases date from the Proto-Palatial Period, deriving their name from the Kamáres cave on the southern flank of the Psilorítis range, where they were first found. The characteristic features are polychrome paintings on a dark background. Motifs from nature such as spirals and rosettes combine to create a harmonious unity.

Neo-Palatial Period vases of the so-called floral style display leaves or other plant motifs, while marine-style vessels are covered with octopuses, paper nautilus or even coral designs. These vessels were either buried with the dead, given as votive offerings or else used as crockery in the palaces where they were found.

though it had been the seat of power for most of southern Crete in Minoan times.

Phaistos is probably the most dramatic Minoan site on the entire island. Its palace is set on top of a rocky knoll with rooms cascading down the hillside. There are sweeping views out across the plain to Mt Psilorítis on the north and the Asteroúsia range to the south. In legend, King Minos installed his brother Rhadamanthys as ruler here. He was known

The Phaistos disc

as a wise and honest man consulted by many as an arbitrator.

The layout of the palace is similar to that of Knossos, but here there has been no reconstruction. Instead, the remains of three successive palaces – two from the Proto-Palatial era and one from the Neo-Palatial era – can be seen, with almost nothing standing more than a metre above the ground. You enter the site down a flight of steps and find yourself in the **west court**, which doubled as a **theatral area**. The remains downhill to the south are of one of the old palaces, just below are the walls of the new palace. You'll see scant remains of a shrine, with kiln-like storage pits whose function is uncertain. On the east side of the west court, the **grand stairway** leads to the **propylon**, the entryway into the newer palace. The **west wing** – as at Knossos – was chiefly made up of shrines and storerooms, and many objects of ritual use were found during excavations here. Some rooms still house their lustral bowls for ritual purification.

Minoan stairway at Agía Triáda

Beyond all this extends the vast **central courtyard** at the southeast corner of the site. From here, you head north towards the royal chambers – two giant *píthi* (large earthenware pots) guard the entryway from the central court. You'll find a peristyle hall here (off limits) and steps leading down to the **King's and Queen's chambers** – both built to make the most of the cooling updrafts of the hillside. The east court was mainly used for practical activities, as there are remnants of a furnace and workshops here – perhaps for copper smelting. They would have supplied the palace with its need for ceremonial or funerary articles.

The **Phaistos disc** was discovered here by workers in 1903 in a tiny, apparently insignificant, clay-walled chamber on the northern edge of the site. The disc, apparently dating from around 1700BC, is covered with a spiral pattern of symbols and geometric forms that have yet to be deciphered. The original lies in Iráklio's Archaeological Museum (see page 36) – though plenty of replicas are on sale at the Phaistos site shop.

AGÍA TRIÁDA AND VÓRI

Just 3km (2 miles) beyond Phaistos on the same road is **Agía Triáda** (daily: summer 8.30am–3.30pm; winter 10am–4pm), built – archeologists believe – as a summer palace for the royal court and linked with Phaistos by Minoan road. Set on a hillside overlooking the Gulf of Mesará it offered excellent views and cooling breezes, as the sea came much closer in those days. The remains indicate modules of rooms that could work either as a whole or individually – perhaps to accommodate varying sizes of entourage at different times. The west wing housed the royal quarters.

Agía Triáda (original name unknown) was built late in the Minoan era, c.1700BC and although it suffered great damage in the cataclysm of 1450BC, it was reoccupied, and a Dorian town was built to one side, its agora still evident. Since the Minoan settlement was famed for several shrines, scholars have debated that the original palace may have had some religious purpose. Numerous tombs have been excavated on the hillside, and the sarcophagus in the Iráklio museum, finely decorated with cult scenes, was found here. Atop the whole site is the incongruous 14th-century church of **Ágios Geórgios** (always open), with fresco fragments inside.

Just 3km from Phaistos, north of the main road, the traditional village of **Vóri** ❻ has clusters of old houses, a central square and an excellent, if spottily labelled, two-storey **Museum of Cretan Ethnology** (www.cretanethnologymuseum.gr; April–Oct daily 11am–5pm; Nov–March by appointment only) near the main church. It's an antique-dealers dream of old furniture, weavings and tools touching on every aspect of rural life, from pig-butchery to bootmaking. Look out for eel traps and animal muzzles made of basketry, an all-wood wheelbarrow and the giant smithy bellows.

MÁTALA TO AGÍA GALÍNI

A more frequented lunch-and-swim stop is the coastal resort of **Mátala** ❼, about 11km (7 miles) southwest of Phaistos. Here you'll find a good sandy bay lined with tavernas. The waters are well regarded by snorkellers and there are fascinating remains of a barely submerged Roman port. On the northern side are high sandstone cliffs where you will find many large **Roman tombs** (daily: April–Sept 10am–7pm; Oct–March 8.30am–3pm) cut into the rock. Until the late 1970s, these man-made caves were unprotected and used as free camping spots by legions of countercultural travellers. Today they are fenced-off and cleared out at dusk.

For a calmer, less commercial alternative, try **Léndas 8** and its long west beach, 23km (14 miles) south from Ágii Déka village beyond the outriders of Asteroúsia. It's too far to fit into most day-outings, so you'll want to spend the night.

Travelling west from the Mesará you'll reach the coastal resort of **Agía Galíni 9**, its buildings tumbling down a hill to a tiny port from which you can take boat excursions along the coast, the best of these to spectacular **Ágios Pávlos** beach, with a huge dune backing it. North from Agía Galíni the main road leads to Réthymno (see page 68).

THE CENTRAL MOUNTAINS

Heading west out of Iráklio you can take the relatively fast New National Road along the coast, with easy links to the resorts of **Agía Pelagía**, **Balí** and (best) **Pánormos**, or the slower Old National Road, which winds its way inland via Damásta and Pérama. The slow route allows you to explore some of the most rugged and interesting landscapes in Crete, and leads you back to mythological times when the gods ruled the earth. The **Psilorítis range 10** dominates central Crete, rising steeply to the chapel of Timiós Stavrós (Holy Cross) on the highest peak – Óros Ídi (Mt Ida) is a distinguished 2,456m (8,056ft) in elevation. In summer the long summit ridge seems almost to touch the clear azure sky; in winter it attracts a mantle of snow and thick menacing clouds, and the foothill villages seem to hang suspended on this swirling grey blanket. Climbing the peak takes around eight hours (round trip) from the Nída Plateau at the base of the ridge, in turn reached on foot from

Zarós or Kamáres, or by path or road from Anógia. Between May and June is the best season, when days are long and snow is minimal. Essential equipment includes Loraine Wilson's *The High Mountains of Crete*, which thoroughly documents all alternatives.

The men and women of this region have been among the most stalwart against Crete's enemies, and subject to some of their worst reprisals – none more so than the inhabitants of the village

Mátala beach and its sandstone cliffs perforated with Roman tombs

of **Anógia ⓫**. The population suffered two bloody occasions under the Ottomans when the village was razed to the ground, and again in World War II. After Cretan and British partisans kidnapped General Kreipe, head of the occupying forces on the island, German soldiers marched into the village, killing all the men and burning houses. Several monuments in the village commemorate these sad events. Through happier times the village has built a reputation for weaving and embroidery – still sold in the lower town – as well as for its musicians (especially the Xylouris clan). This is one place where you will probably see men in their traditional costume of *stivánia* (high leather boots), *vrákes* (baggy breeches) and *saríki* (headband).

Anógia, on a separate secondary route above the old national road, is a popular point of entry to Psilorítis. Follow a paved road out of the top of the village towards the Nída Plateau, once visited only by shepherds tending their flocks. From there, it's only

Crete's caves

There are more than 3,000 caves in Crete – approximately half of all the caves in Greece. This is due to the porous, water-soluble properties of the island's limestone strata.

a short walk to the **Idaean Cave** (Idéon Andron) where in legend the god Zeus spent his childhood, protected from his father Kronos by fierce, shield-banging warriors, the *kouretes*. Though the cave itself is not very impressive, it held a powerful sway over its ancient people; archeologists have found votive offerings dating back over 3,000 years.

EASTERN CRETE

This part of Crete offers contrasting landscapes. Some of the longest-established resorts sprawl along the northern coast, while inland, verdant valleys divide mountain ranges that were trackless until the 1970s. Here, it is still just possible to find the traditional rural lifestyle once omnipresent in the interior of the island.

Caves, gorges and a smattering of ancient sites add to the attraction, and make the east a good location for a combination beach/excursion holiday.

ROWDY RESORTS

Heading out from Iráklio, you'll pass the airport some 5km (3 miles) away before reaching the beginning of the coastal strip. The New National Road takes you swiftly along, so if you want to explore, take the Old National Road where it still exists. This part of the northern coast was the main target of development during the 1970s and 1980s, and it is not to everyone's taste. Large concrete hotels and apartments make up a home from home for many European nationals, with English, German and Dutch menus,

satellite football and all the favourite northern European TV pro-
grammes. At times it's hard to believe that you are on a Greek
island. However, if you want almost nonstop fun, then this is the
place for you. Waterparks, bungee-jumping, go-karting, bars and
nightclubs – it's all here.

MÁLIA TO NEÁPOLI

En route to Mália you may want to visit the **Lychnostatis open-air
museum** (Hersonisso; www.lychnostatis.gr; Sun–Fri 9am–2pm),
which is dedicated to Cretan flora, folk art and ethnography.
The development reaches a peak at **Liménas Hersonísou ⑫**,
although the inland village of **Ano Hersónisos** still has vestiges
of its old atmosphere – and some Cretan tavernas. Liménas
rivals **Mália ⑬** as the island's clubbing capital, famous for fine
beaches and also home to
the tranquil Minoan **Palace
of Mália** (bit.ly/MaliaPalace;
summer Wed–Mon 8am–
6pm; winter Wed–Mon
8am–3.30pm), in farmland
close to the sea around 2km
(1 mile) east of town.

Remains under and
around the palace indi-
cate Neolithic settlements,
although the first palace
was built after 2000BC
(later than Knossos and
Phaistos) and it revealed
no Kamáresware pottery
from the Pre-Palatial period
like that found at the other

*The bare mountains
and verdant valleys of
Eastern Crete*

palaces. Its design is also simpler, with no large halls or fine wall decorations. This first palace was destroyed by an earthquake *c*.1700BC; there are scant remains of it on the northwest of the site.

The new palace centred on an open courtyard with a **west wing** mainly consisting of storerooms and cult rooms. A loggia fronted the square on this wing. In one room a *píthos* was found with a ceremonial dagger inside, and alongside this lay a sword decorated with gold and crystal, leading scholars to conclude that this was a preparation or contemplation room for the king. Up a nearby flight of stairs is an **altar room** with the base of its altar table still in situ.

Further west a *polythron* area with a paved floor is thought to have been the **royal apartments**. Hieroglyphic clay tablets and official seals were found here. Just a little way north of the palace site is the **chrysólakkos** or 'pit of gold', a mausoleum where the much-prized golden bee pendant was discovered among a larger cache of jewels. Archeologists are now busy excavating the extensive town that surrounded the palace and parts of this – on the palace's northwest flank – can be viewed from an overhead walkway.

Soon after ancient Mália the road turns inland past the town of **Neápoli**, birthplace of Petros Philargos, who, raised as a Catholic, became Pope Alexander V in 1409 – or rather, the Pisan 'antipope', as there were three rival claimants to the papacy at the time. This is the only place on the island where you can try *soumáda*, a sweet drink made from wild almonds. It was capital of Lasíthi district before Ágios Nikólaos, and still marks the start of a scenic road up to the eponymous plateau.

ÁGIOS NIKÓLAOS

Eventually new and old highways meet the coast again at **Ágios Nikólaos** ⑭, probably the pleasantest town in eastern Crete. Though Agios Nikólaos – known to many Brits as 'Ag Nik' – suffered from a rash of ugly buildings going up in the 1970s, it has since made an effort to retain its character, and offers a more Greek atmosphere than the Mália/Liménas Hersonísou strip.

The town sits on the **Gulf of Mirabéllo**, blanketing low hills that rise up from the shoreline. At the centre of town is **Lake Voulisméni**, a 60-metre-deep spring-fed lake where a plethora of pretty fishing boats are tied. Numerous cafés and tavernas line the north and eastern edges of the lake, and you can sit and watch kingfishers swoop for minnows or divers descend to the bluey-green depths.

The south and west sides of the lake are flanked by sheer rock faces and you can climb the steps to the top for superb views over the town – perfect at sunset.

Lake Voulisméni is connected to the sea by an artificial channel. Across the road bridge at its mouth is the main tourist office, and

Píthi amongst the ruins of Mália's Minoan palace

beyond is the main port – where ferries no longer call. From the quay just beyond the bridge, excursion boats ply to local attractions, though it's a very long way to Spinalónga (see page 57).

You won't be able to explore Ágios Nikólaos without climbing a few hills. Shops selling upmarket clothing line the harbourside and Mt Skafianá, leading to Kitroplatía cove. Part-pedestrianised Ikosiogdóis Oktovríou makes for another pleasant stroll towards the central plaza.

The local **Archaeological Museum**, (closed for renovation at the time of writing, check website before visiting; bit.ly/ArchAgios) near the top of Konstandínou Paleológou keeps a good collection of Minoan artefacts, presented in chronological order. You may view a sarcophagus with skeleton still in place, and the 'Goddess of Myrtos', an exquisite libation vessel dating from the 2nd millennium BC in the shape of a woman with a long neck and squat body. A later Roman find is the skull from Potamós, decorated with a crown of gold olive leaves. The coin nearby was found between the skull's teeth, presumably the dead man's fare to the ferryman across the River Styx to the underworld.

ELOÚNDA TO SPINALÓNGA ISLAND

Ágios Nikólaos does not have great beaches; Havánia just west of town, and Almyrós 2km (1 mile) south, are serviceable at best. As a consequence, much of its upmarket accommodation lies north along the coast towards **Káto Eloúnda**. This coastal resort is understated, with a pretty church on the waterfront. You can also head to Spinalónga island from here – a much shorter trip than from Ágios Nikólaos. Don't confuse it with Cape Spinalónga, accessible from Eloúnda via a narrow causeway over an artificial canal.

In the shallows around the causeway are the remains of the Greco-Roman city of **Oloús**, still flourishing during the 2nd century AD, according to Greek geographer Pausanias. It probably sank during tectonic upheavals in the 4th century, which did spare an early Christian basilica (fenced off) inland, whose floor mosaics include frolicking dolphins.

Still further north on the mainland, the tiny coastal resort of **Pláka** has the quickest, cheapest boat transfer (9am–6pm every half hour in season) to Spinalónga island, directly offshore. Weekends are very busy – best to embark before 11am – and take a hat and liquids as there's no shade or refreshment on the island.

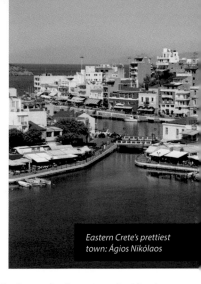

Eastern Crete's prettiest town: Ágios Nikólaos

Spinalónga island ⓑ (April–Oct daily 8.30am–6pm; Nov–March closed except to arranged groups) is girded with the bastions and curtain walls of the Venetian stronghold, built in 1579 to protect the entrance to the sheltered bay behind; a late Ottoman town on the sheltered, landward side; and the leper colony that later occupied it. The fortress was never taken by force; the Venetian garrison remained here until 1715, over 60 years after the fall of Iráklio, and left only after a treaty gave them safe passage. Muslim Cretans in turn retreated to the island when they came under threat from Cretan rebels at the end of the 19th century.

In 1903, the Cretan administrative council decided to establish a leper colony here; whether this was to force the Muslim villagers to leave is debatable, but the disease was rampant on the main island, and Spinalónga's position – offshore yet not too remote – was considered ideal for quarantining its sufferers. Initially, the

Spinalónga's former leper colony

regime was harsh, with victims treated more like criminals than patients; however, conditions improved over the years, thanks to patient activism and a new medication regime after 1948, until the colony was disbanded in 1957. Allow at least 90 minutes to explore the fortifications and the old town. Part of the old market street has been restored, the renovated shops now house an interesting museum.

INLAND TO KRITSÁ

Inland from Ágios Nikólaos are three attractions that fill an enjoyable morning or afternoon of sightseeing. Head out towards the village of Kritsá 12km (7 miles) from town. Before you reach the village itself you'll find a beautiful Byzantine chapel on the right. **Panagía Kerá ⑯** (Wed–Mon 8.30am–3.30pm) was built in the 13th century and decorated with superb frescoes of the 14th and 15th centuries. You'll need time, and the guide booklet on sale, to take in every detail of the interior. Although many frescoes are damaged or uncleaned, existing highlights include a 'Presentation of the Virgin' and 'Last Supper' in the vault of the main nave, and the 'Water of Proof' in the south aisle.

Resume your journey toward Kritsá, but don't visit the village just yet. Instead, follow signs 4km (2.5 miles) along a side road to **Lató** (free access), the remains of a Dorian city (7th–3rd centuries BC) scattered around two scrub-covered hilltops to the north.

Finally, allow yourself to head into **Kritsá** for some well-earned refreshments and rest. This 'traditional' village is perhaps overly touristy for some, but it is still very much lived-in and extremely well kept, with brilliant-whitewashed walls accented by colourful window frames and potted plants. Good tavernas can be found near the old village square – distinguished by its huge plane tree. Famed for its carpet weaving and textiles, you'll also see them hanging from walls and shop doorways in the narrow streets.

THE LASÍTHI PLATEAU

If Kritsá is a good example of a hill-village 'rescued' by tourism, others have seen their rural economy collapse since the 1970s. Travelling inland toward the towering peaks of the **Díkti Mountains** brings you to a region that was isolated from the rest of Crete, except by horse or donkey travel, until well after World War II. Improved access to the **Lasíthi Plateau** ⓱ (Oropédio Lasithíou) ironically just accelerated the depopulation.

OVERNIGHT SENSATION

The 2010 Greek television series *To Nisi* (The Island), based on Victoria Hislop's novel of that name, has been a huge success, resulting in a continuing traffic of Greek visitors to the Spinalónga area. It was shot mostly at Pláka and the hillside village of Páno Eloúnda, as the archeological authorities did not let Mega Cannel's crews use the island itself as a location. The sets at Pláka are now dismantled, but at Páno Eloúnda they have been left as a tourist attraction, cleverly intermingled with the original houses. Wandering the attractive streets, you can see why the village, with its sweeping views, was chosen.

Two main roads climb up to 850m (2,800ft) altitude. From the New Road above Mália you head through the tiny settlements of **Krási**, with an ancient plane tree gracing the main square, and **Kerá**, where you can visit 14th-century **Panagía Kardiotíssis** (Our Lady of the Heart) before proceeding through the dramatic **Séli Ambélou Pass** with its ruined stone windmills.

Or you can ascend from Neápoli on a longer road not used by tour coaches, through the little oases of **Exo** and **Mésa Potámi**, for a panoramic initial view of the plain and the impressive **Psarí Madára** peak (2,148m/7,047ft) beyond.

A single road circles the plain, linking together all the small communities, though you'll find many of their houses derelict or rented by Romani people, and their shops shuttered since the flight down the mountain. What agricultural activity that still persists is often much delayed lately by heavy spring rains, as the valley floor drains slowly. Potatoes and grain grow on the plateau, with sheep grazing the stubble; orchards (especially apples and cherries) and silver-leaved vines are cultivated on the surrounding slopes.

The famous windmills, which used to pump up water in late spring, have now mostly vanished; just a few at the north edge of the plateau are left spinning idly for show, their pistons disconnected and storage tanks empty.

On the southern edge of the plain, 1km (0.5 miles) above **Psyhró** village where powerful springs nourish a plane tree, yawns the large **Dictean Cave** (Diktéon Andron; daily: summer 8am–8pm; winter 8am–3pm), said to be the birthplace of Zeus. Ancient votive offerings left in the cave confirm that it was revered during Minoan times.

It is a 15-minute walk (or expensive mule ride) from the parking lot. From the entrance, the cave drops precipitously 65m (215ft) into the cavern. Try to spot the monstrous face of Kronos, eating his new offspring Zeus, and the small nipple-shaped stalagmites on which the infant god is said to have suckled.

EAST TO SITÍA

Heading east from Ágios Nikólaos, the new road along the northern coast is still in the throes of construction. Follow the gulf initially south to **Ístro** where there is a garland of beaches (best of these being **Voúlisma**), and then east to one of the major ancient sites locally – **Gourniá** ⑱, 18km (11 miles) from Ágios Nikólaos (Tues–Sun 8am–3pm). Myriad stone walls – foundations for multi-storeyed homes – linked by cobbled streets blanket the hillside. Here, more than at any other Minoan site, it is possible to envision ordinary people going about their daily business. You may also explore the marketplace and small workshops of the artisans.

The palace sat at the top of the hill, its west court housing a sacrificial slab and storerooms for ritual liquids and libations as seen in other Minoan palaces. Gourniá was a large city, stretching all the way down to the coast where it had an important and busy port. However, much remains to be uncovered. The best overview of Gourniá – excavated by American Harriet Boyd Hawkes in the early 1900s – is from the main road as it rises beyond the archeological site.

Whitewashed walls of mountainous Kritsá

From Gourniá the Old National Road traces a tortuous course, via sleepy hill-villages towards Sitía. The one spot of note actually on the coast, down one of two side roads, is **Móhlos** ⑲, now an easygoing resort on a cape despite lacking a beach, but during Minoan times an important site. The Minoan settlement sits on a small island just 150m (480ft) offshore – you can take a boat or swim across to reach it – although it was connected to the mainland 3,000 years ago. A little way offshore to the west is **Psíra**, for which you will definitely need boat transportation to visit the Minoan port town.

Eventually the northern road drops into **Sitía** ⑳, a bustling port town of about 9,000 people – including students at the local geological school and police academy, who keep the waterfront bars and *ouzerís* lively all year.

Tiers of houses rise from Sitía's waterfront

A Minoan settlement at **Petrás** lies 1km (0.5 miles) to the east, but the Venetians chose this hillside location, building a fortress – the **Kazárma** – on its highest point. Unfortunately the Turks destroyed the Venetian domestic buildings when they took the town but a network of narrow lanes and stone steps spill down to a waterfront promenade, and these have delightful architectural and lifestyle details to discover. Sitía also has a pleasing **Archaeological Museum** (bit.ly/SitiaMuseum; Wed–Mon 8.30am–3.30pm) displaying finds mostly from Zákros, in particular a large collection of painted *lárnakes* (clay burial chambers), as well as a ceramic wine press and *souvláki* grill. You'll find it just south of the town centre.

TOPLOÚ TO ZÁKROS

Sitía is the gateway to the far east of Crete. Now sparsely populated, with most villages located inland and subsisting on olives and grapes, this region conceals important Minoan sites suggesting that many people lived here 3,000 years ago. For those who want to explore the area there's plenty of accommodation around Palékastro and Káto Zákros. Surprisingly, in this remote part of the island a procession of tour buses arrives every day from Ágios Nikólaos and beyond.

Many of these are headed for one of Crete's most influential religious institutions, **Moní Toploú ㉑** (Toploú Monastery; daily 9am–1pm, 2–6pm; Oct–Mar until 4pm), an oasis in an otherwise rather bleak landscape, owned almost entirely by the Orthodox Church. Founded in the 14th century, the monastery was built for contemplation, but also for protection against outside threats. Toploú is a Turkish word meaning 'with cannon' – the more correct title for the monastery is Kyriá Akrotirianí – indicating that the abbots were no timorous recluses. Its walls suggest more a fortress than a religious refuge – though even these were not enough to protect it from being sacked by pirates in 1498. The monastery played a signal role in Cretan uprisings against the Turks – 12 monks were hanged in 1821 – and more recently against the Germans in World War II when it was a safe-house for British soldiers and native partisans. The abbot and several monks were shot in reprisal before the war's end.

The monastery church and museum shelters many treasures, foremost among them the intricate 18th-century icon by Ioannis Kornaros, with 61 miniature scenes based on the Orthodox prayer 'Lord, Thou Art Great'; at its top is a finely wrought Holy Trinity, framed rather bizarrely by zodiacal signs. There are also two galleries of strange and rare engravings, plus illuminated gospels. Sadly, most of the monastery, other than the courtyard, is now off-limits. In the extensive gift shop, you can buy reproductions of the icon or olive oil produced from the monks' own groves. September 26 is the monastery's celebration day, attracting many pilgrims to the site.

Northeast of Toploú awaits one of Crete's natural wonders. Amid arid scenery, a grove of verdant date palms appears, with beyond a swathe of blond sand lapped by azure waters. This is **Váï ㉒**, extremely beautiful and correspondingly popular at peak season, when it's absolutely packed. The palms are claimed to have grown from pips spat out by Arab pirates, though the less romantic truth is that they're an indigenous variety *(Phoenix theophrastii)* that have been present here for millennia. If Váï is 'full', retire instead to three less crowded sandy coves 3km (2 miles) north at **Itanos** – there are date palms here too at the southerly cove.

From both Váï and Toploú roads converge on modern **Palékastro** village, with the Minoan site of Rousolakkos nearby (still being excavated, free access), overlooking Hióna beach, the ancient port. This is separated by a headland from superior **Kouremén os ㉓** beach with its windsurfing facilities.

South from Palékastro, the narrower road shies away from the coast, threading villages that are trailheads for great hikes, including through two gorges: the **Hohlahiés canyon**, ending at isolated Karoúmes beach, and the more famous **Zákros Gorge** (better known as the **Valley of the Dead**). Either take about 90 minutes going downhill (2 hours up), with year-round drinking water in the 'Deads' Gorge' (as it's signposted locally). Your reward, at the bottom of **Zákros ㉔**, is a Minoan palace and another long beach with several tavernas.

The **Palace of Zákros** (daily: summer 8am–8pm; winter 8.30am–3.30pm) sits just behind this strand on flat ground, with its associated town flanking it on the hillside. With its large port, Zákros was well situated for trade with Egypt and Syria. Building began around 1900BC, though these remains are now invisible owing to subsidence. The exposed, second palace was completed c.1600BC, but the cataclysm of 1450BC saw a sudden abandonment of the city; it was never resettled.

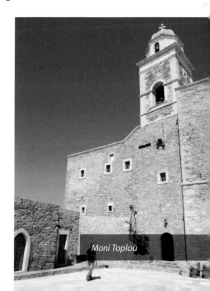

The **west wing** of the palace was mostly devoted to cult practices, with workshops in the south. The **north wing** housed the royal entourage and the main kitchen, while the east was reserved for the royal apartments. Archeologists discovered treasures in many of these rooms.

Moní Toploú

One unique aspect of Zákros is the east wing's water feature, behind the royal apartments. The **cistern hall** contains a circular cistern, still full of water, now inhabited by Caspian pond terrapins. Nearby, the ceremonial 'built fountain' has steps descending to a small, square pool.

THE SOUTHEASTERN COAST

At **Xérokambos**, the next shoreline settlement beyond Káto Zákros, the road turns inland to arrive dramatically at upland **Zíros** village; the coast below is either inaccessible by car or unrewarding if you do get to it. At Zíros you might prefer to stay inland, meeting the main road south from Sitía just past **Etiá** Ⓟ, a Venetian-founded village, now abandoned, with a rare and superbly restored Venetian manor-house (Tues–Sun 8.30am–3pm) contain-

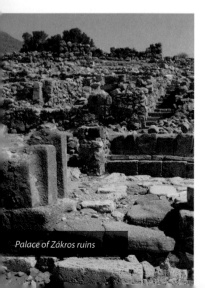

Palace of Zákros ruins

ing a worthwhile display on life in Venetian Crete.

However you travel, the next reasonable halting-point is **Makrý Gialós** Ⓠ, a low-key if straggly resort with an equally long, gently shelving beach and portside tavernas. From here west the coast is more populated, with pine trees and small sandy bays (the most scenic of these **Agía Fotiá** and **Ahliá**) en route to Ierápetra, also reachable by a direct (but dull) road across the narrowest point of Crete from near Gourniá.

Ierápetra **㉗** is the fourth-largest settlement on Crete and claims to be the southernmost town in Europe. As ancient Ierapytna, it was the last Cretan city to fall to the Romans, who used it as a base for their conquest of Egypt. Today Ierápetra is a thriving agricultural-supply centre, enveloped in ranks of plastic greenhouses, with a resort tacked on to the east almost as an afterthought. The limited list of conventional tourist attractions in the small old quarter comprises a tiny Venetian castle (Tues–Sun 8am–3pm, but subject to change), an 18th-century mosque with truncated minaret and a small archeological 'collection' (Tues–Sun 8am–3pm) inside a former Koranic school.

Zákros treasures

Zákros, the last Minoan settlement to be excavated (in the 1960s), revealed a wealth of undisturbed artefacts. Tools and ceremonial objects were found just where they were dropped at the time of the great cataclysm, along with the crystal rhyton on view in the Iráklio Museum and a chest containing hundreds of clay tablets inscribed with Linear A script. Archeologists even discovered an urn with olives preserved through the millennia.

West of Ierápetra, the greenhouses have mostly vanished by the time you reach **Mýrtos** **㉘**, 16km (10 miles) along, a laid-back, slightly 'alternative' resort just beyond the Minoan sites of Foúrnou Korýfi and Pýrgos. Despite German destruction in late 1943 as reprisal for resistance activity, it's a cheerful, welcoming place, almost a proper town, with a long beach and the Nikos Kazantzakis Museum (www.kazantzaki.gr; April–Oct daily 9am–5pm; Nov–March Sun–Fri 10am–3pm). The author of *Zorba the Greek* was born in Iráklio in 1885. If for any reason Mýrtos doesn't suit, continue 5km (3 miles) west to **Tértsa**, another long beach

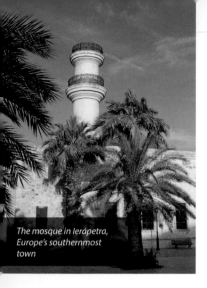

The mosque in Ierápetra, Europe's southernmost town

with the summits of the Díkti range visible overhead. With a car, make the trip west and inland (33km/21 miles) to **Áno Viánnos 29**, a surprisingly large village in the Díkti foothills overlooking a fertile plain. The big attraction here is a tiny 14th-century **Agía Pelagía** church up the hill (well signposted, always open), with idiosyncratic frescoes from the life of Christ. From here it's easy to continue on into Iráklio district.

WESTERN CRETE

Western Crete offers a diverse range of attractions: two delightful towns on the north coast, unspoiled mountains where you can hike or experience Cretan rural life, tiny south-coast villages reached only on foot or by boat. This area is less densely populated than Iráklio district and has more rainfall, making it more lushly vegetated. These contrasts make it a fascinating part of the island to spend a vacation.

Réthymno 30 lies 75km (50 miles) west of Iráklio, one hour away along the New National Road. The site has been settled since Minoan times, with Dorian, Greek and Roman remains underlying the present town. Venetian rule spawned many of the architectural gems here, although evidence of the Ottoman period also abounds. Réthymno suffered many attacks and sackings over the

THE SOUTHEASTERN COAST | 69

centuries. Much of the town was badly damaged in the battle for Crete during World War II, although the old quarter survived. Today, a modern tourist district extends to the east, taking advantage of the long sandy bay, but this has not spoilt the old town, a delightful place in which to stroll.

Réthymno has also been the intellectual centre of Crete throughout the ages, and is home to the island's most esteemed university. Annually in July the town attracts artists from across Greece for its Renaissance Festival.

The old town occupies a strategic nub of land jutting out from the long, flat coastline. A huge fortress – the **Fortezza** (daily 10am–6pm) – dominates the site, its walls rising high above the streets on the northwestern point. This is considered to be the largest fortification ever built by the Venetians, who completed the task in 1580. The finest views of the walls are from the waterfront promenade outside, from where you can appreciate its grand scale.

Once inside, it is easy to imagine a large garrison stationed here, with the ruins of barracks and arsenals scattered everywhere. Right at the heart of it is the restored, 1647-built **Mosque of Ibrahim Han**, the largest domed structure in Greece, now hosting concerts or art exhibits. Despite its strength and dominant position, Ottoman forces made

Ierápetra day trip

From Ierápetra's jetty you can take a trip to Hrissí (Gaïdouro) islet, some 7 nautical miles offshore but plainly visible on the horizon. This nearly flat islet is covered in rare junipers and has at least two white-sand beaches. In season it's possible to eat lunch in the harbour's tavern. Excursion boats leave in the summer every half-hour from 10.30am until 12pm, returning from Hrissí in the afternoon.

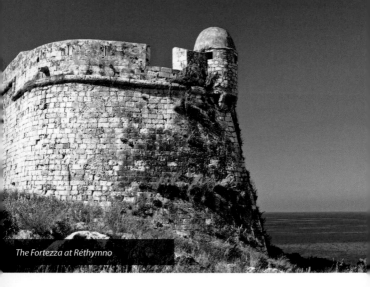

The Fortezza at Réthymno

surprisingly light work of taking the fortress in 1646 – they simply landed elsewhere on the coast and then invaded the town from the land.

Walking downhill from the fortress gate brings you to the enchanting **Venetian inner harbour**, now a haven for small fishing craft and excursion boats, guarded by a 19th-century lighthouse at the end of the stone jetty. The harbour cafés where Ottoman Cretans used to socialise over coffee and shared *nargilédes* (hubble-bubbles) have now become somewhat touristy tavernas.

Behind the old harbour the maze of narrow, mostly pedestrianised streets, ideal for strolling, forms the core of the old quarter. The most obvious sight will be shopping opportunities at eye level: craft and jewellery stores create tempting displays, and cotton clothing is swathed across every wall.

However, don't neglect to look behind the merchandise to see Venetian stone lintels above, or to glimpse ornate Ottoman *kióskia* (enclosed wooden balconies) or entire housefronts draped in bougainvillaea. At night the streets come alive with shoppers and revellers, and excellent restaurants occupy some of the old buildings.

If you exit the harbour from the southwest, you cross busy Arkadíou towards the **Venetian Loggia**, built in 1600. It has been rescued from years of dereliction, now housing an upmarket gallery where you can buy excellent copies of museum pieces. Walk down Paleológou to find the still-flowing **Rimondi Fountain**. Built in the 1620s, its lion-head spouts have taken on an aged patina and it looks strangely out of place in this bustling square.

From here the principal shopping street, Ethnikís Antistáseos, leads south. Turn right onto Vernárdou where you will immediately find the **Nerantzés Mosque** (Tzamí ton Nerantzión), a converted Venetian church – something obvious from the north portal – now used as a conservatory and concert hall. Beyond this the **Historical and Folklore Museum** (April–Oct Mon–Sat 9am–2.30pm), in a fine old Venetian mansion, provides an evocative glimpse of bygone Crete. The upstairs galleries feature embroidery, weavings, farm and kitchen implements and ceramics. Situated on the same street is also the **Museum of Contemporary Art of Crete** (Himaras 5; www.cca.gr; May–Oct Tues–Fri 9am–2pm and 7–9pm, Sat & Sun 10am–3pm; Nov–April Tues–Fri 9am–2pm, Wed & Fri also 6–9pm, Sat & Sun 10am–3pm). The permanent exhibition showcases works from contemporary Greek artists.

Ethnikís Antistáseos soon ends at the **Porta Goura**; this stone gateway, all that remains of the original town walls, separates the old quarter from the traffic-filled 21st century just beyond. Across the busy boulevard is the tempting shade of the **Municipal Gardens**, formerly a Muslim cemetery. Within ten minutes' walk of the Gardens is the recently relocated **Archaeological Museum** (Saint Francis Church; Saint Francis 4; www.archmuseumreth. gr; daily: April–Oct 9am–5pm; Nov–March 8.30am–3.30pm) displaying late Minoan and Roman finds including clay sarcophagi painted with stylised animals.

SOUTH OF RÉTHYMNO

The area south of Réthymno is well worth exploring by car, but its major attraction can be visited by public or tour bus. **Moní Arkadíou** ㉛ (Arkádi Monastery; www.arkadimonastery.gr; daily: March & Oct 9am–6pm; April, May & Sept 9am–7pm; June–Aug 9am–8pm; Nov 9am–5pm) lies in the Psilorítis foothills some 23km (14 miles) southeast of Réthymno. It was founded in the Byzantine era, although its present buildings date from the late 16th century and is revered by Cretans as a nationalist shrine.

In 1866 the Orthodox islanders rebelled yet once more against Ottoman rule. As the attempt failed, hundreds of partisans sought sanctuary in the compound. The Muslims demanded their surrender and, when Abbot Gavriíl (Gabriel) refused, they besieged the monastery.

On 9 November the attackers breached the outer walls to find the Greeks barricaded in a wine depot, where they had also stored their gunpowder. As the Ottoman forces made their way toward this last refuge, the abbot ordered the explosives to be fired. The resulting blast killed hundreds of defenders and attackers, giving real meaning to the battle cry of Crete – 'freedom or death'.

Today, the monastery is a much more peaceful place, although the fateful storeroom remains a charred shell. The Venetian-style church gracing the middle of the compound is one of the most beautiful on Crete. Its façade of yellow sandstone is richly carved with a fine belfry, and mock Corinthian columns dignify each of the twin entranceways.

From **Moní Arkadíou**, it is only about six kilometres east to the recently inaugurated **Museum of Ancient Eleutherna** (https://mae.uoc.gr; Wed–Mon 10am–6pm). The collection consists of three rooms. Room A presents the everyday life in ancient Eleutherna. Room B and C show respectively the religious practices and burial customs of the site's community from the Iron Age to the Byzantine era.

Southeast of Réthymno lie two valleys leading towards the far coast. The **Amári Valley** ㉜ is the more easterly and the more exciting, with traditional rural landscapes to explore and dramatic views of Psilorítis

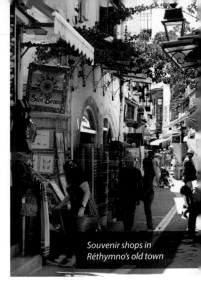

Souvenir shops in Réthymno's old town

as a backdrop. You'll need a car or mountain bike, as public buses or tours here are non-existent, and accommodation scarce. The main valley loop road leads through a string of small villages, many graced with fine old, frescoed churches, and all with memorials commemorating the 1944 German reprisals exacted for resistance operations.

At **Thrónos**, the 11th-century **Panagía chapel** has superb, later frescoes – the shop next door keeps the key (daily 9am–6pm; a tip is expected). The adjacent hamlet of **Kalógeros** has the small **Theológos chapel**, with more 14th-century frescoes. **Monastiráki**, southeast of here, offers two more churches: tiny **Aï Geórgi**, at the top of the village, with a fine image of the Panagía Platytéra, and Venetian-style **Arhángelos** (key from café opposite) retains a fresco of the Dormition. East from here, **Platánia** has another Panagía chapel (key from nearby café) with a vivid, nearly complete cycle of frescoes, some unusual – note the rarely shown

> **Water feature**
>
> There are several other fountains, now dry but inscribed with elegant Ottoman calligraphy, scattered across town. The easiest to find are alongside the multi-domed Kara Pasha Mosque and on the corner of Smýrnis and Koronéou, below the Fortezza.

Angel Gabriel, and St George with a right earring in the Byzantine manner. Going instead anticlockwise from Thrónos, **Méronas** offers the **Metamórfosi chapel** by the school, with well-preserved scenes of St Stephen and the Transfiguration, but the central village church of **Panagía**, with the most complete fresco cycle in the valley, is only rarely opened by the priest.

The second valley to the west leads up to the little hill-town of **Spíli**. Stop to sample the central **Venetian fountain** – a series of 30 kitsch-modern lion-heads spouting crystal clear, cool water from Mt Kédros overhead – before exploring the backstreets. The **Folk Museum of Spili** (daily 10am–6pm), within a short walk of the fountain, is also worth a visit. The small exhibition contains tools that used to be owned by the members of the local community and gives an idea of how a traditional Cretan house would have looked.

THE SOUTH COAST

Beyond Spíli the main road heads east towards Agía Galíni (see page 50), but turn right 6km (4 miles) before Spíli to pass through the dramatic **Kourtaliótiko Gorge** en route to Plakiás and Préveli Monastery on the south coast.

Moní Préveli ③ (Préveli Monastery; www.preveli.org; daily: May–Sept 9am–1.30pm, 3.30–6.30pm; Oct–April 9am–5pm) is a remote religious community and, like most others, was involved in partisan activities during Crete's struggles for freedom. The fathers helped many Allied prisoners to escape in World War II, while an earlier monastery (Káto Préveli – you pass the evocative but fenced-off ruins en route) was sacked in 1821. Newer Préveli dates from the 17th century and was the richest religious house in Crete during the Ottoman era. Its church contains a splendid iconostasis, considered the best on the island, while in the small treasury museum a gold and diamond crucifix purportedly contains a piece of the True Cross.

Below the monastery, a steep track descends to the car park for '**Palm Beach**', a sandy, stream-fed cove from which the World War II evacuations took place.

In the other direction, west along the coast, minor roads lead to **Plakiás** ㉞ and beyond. Plakiás is a burgeoning resort situated along a crescent-shaped bay, though better beaches flank it at **Damnóni** and **Ammoúdi** to the east, and **Soúda** on the west.

West over the border in Haniá district, the walls of **Frangokástello** ㉟ can be seen rising behind a sandy beach. This dramatic 14th-century fortress is now just an empty shell – like a set for a film about the French Foreign Legion. The Venetians built it not only to ward off pirates but to intimidate Cretan fighters in the mountains behind.

Moní Arkadíou, a national Cretan shrine

During Ottoman rule Frangokástello was the scene of many critical events, including the capture of the rebel Daskalogiannis in 1770 and the massacre of 700 Cretans in 1828.

This secondary coast road ends at Komitádes, just beyond which stands **Hóra Sfakión ㊱**, a little port resort that was the main Allied evacuation point after the Battle of Crete in 1941; a memorial commemorates the event. The road veers inland towards **Anópoli**, and coastal points west of Hóra can only be reached by boat or on foot. Boats pick hikers up from the base of the Samariá Gorge, and at busy times rows of tour buses await here to whisk them away. You can take boat trips to inhabited **Gávdos** islet, the most southern territory in Europe, or to nearby **Loutró**, a picturesque village with no vehicular access; alternatively, you can hike west along the E4 trail to Loutró, Anópoli and many points beyond.

From Komitádes, the main road follows the spectacular **Imbros Gorge ㊲**, with its rich flora and fauna. This gorge is easier than the nearby Samariá, and you can descend it (takes 2.5 hrs approximately) by leaving your car at the village of Ímbros. **Komitádes** marks the bottom, where you can take an afternoon bus or taxi back to your start point.

RÉTHYMNO TO HANIÁ

The coastline between Réthymno and Haniá has its share of resorts, although sandy coves are not the rule. An exception is **Georgioúpoli ㊳**, with a long, sandy beach demarcated by a river on the west. Its best feature, however, is nearby **Lake Kourná**, the only freshwater lake in Crete, surprisingly large, with idyllic swimming and pedalos or kayaks to rent.

Northeast from here, via the characterful inland village of **Vámos, Kalýves** and **Almyrída** are the busiest spots. All roads emerge at **Soúda Bay**, home of Crete's largest port and one of the Mediterranean's best deepwater anchorages. It is the port for

Haniá, with ferry services to Piraeus, while the Greek Navy shares a large base here with NATO. The **British Commonwealth War cemetery** can be found at the head of the bay.

The **Akrotíri Peninsula** ㊟ flanks Soúda on the north. Here you'll find Haniá's airport, several small villages and beaches, plus three important monasteries. Seventeenth-century **Agía Triáda** (aka Zangarolón; daily: summer 8am–sunset;

Kourtaliótiko Gorge

winter 8am–2pm, 4pm–sunset) is today largely a museum, the most imposing item its Venetian façade, with a small shop selling monastic wine and olive oil. More isolated **Gouvernétou Monastery** 4km (2.5 miles) north is a functioning monastery not open to non-Orthodox, but it marks the start of the strenuous, two-hour (round trip) hike down to the evocative remains of **Katholikó**, Crete's first monastery, founded in the 11th century by St John the Hermit. Set on the side of a rocky ravine, it was abandoned during the 17th century in response to pirate raids in favour of Gouvernétou.

As you head towards Haniá, stop at the **tombs of Eleftherios Venizelos** (1864–1936), Crete's greatest statesman, and of his son Sophokles. On this spot, on the orders of Eleftherios Venizelos, the Greek flag was raised in 1897 in defiance of ongoing negotiations amongst the major European powers about the fate of Crete. There are wonderful views across the bay to Haniá, and an adjacent bar from which to enjoy them.

HANIÁ

The capital of Crete from 1845 until 1971, **Haniá** �40 remains the island's second-largest settlement, and despite extensive modern development at the outskirts, remains an immediately likeable place, currently more prosperous than Iráklio, and one of the few cities where Greeks from elsewhere choose to live. At its heart is a delightful old town replete with Venetian and Ottoman buildings and full of cosmopolitan atmosphere, considered to be one of the most beautiful in the whole of Greece.

The **Venetian harbour** attracts visitors and locals alike. It is huge by comparison with Réthymno's, with outer and inner sections. The waterfront is lined with beautiful medieval buildings and numerous cafés and tavernas, an evening lodestar of attraction. The faded stucco of the harbour buildings takes on a delicate rosy hue as night falls, contrasting with the deep blue sky.

The **Firkás bastion** at the northwest corner of the outer harbour is a Venetian ramparts housing the **Maritime Museum of Crete** ⓐ (Naftikó Mousío; www.mar-mus-crete.gr; Mon–Sat: May–Oct 9am–4pm; Nov–April 9am–3pm), which displays shells, model ships, maps and naval paraphernalia. Walk through the archway beyond the museum entrance for views east across the harbour from the bastion. Nearby on Theotokopoúlou, the Venetian church of San Salvatore shelters the well-designed **Byzantine and Post-Byzantine**

MISTS OR MYSTERIES?

Every year in mid-May local people living near Frangokástello say that they can see the spirits of the dead rebels from 1828 marching around the base of the castle. These *drosoulítes* or 'dewy ones' rise from the morning mists, and meteorologists assure us that they are simply a form of weather phenomena, not phantasms.

Collection  (bit.ly/
ChaniaMuseum; Wed–Mon
8.30am–3.30pm), with icons
of the Cretan School, jewellery, coins, a floor mosaic and
fresco fragments rescued
from nearby country chapels.

If you walk down to the
sea from here, you can follow partly pedestrianised
Pireós inland along the finest surviving section of the
old city walls, ending at the
massive **Skhiávo bastion**
🄲. Staying instead by the
sea leads to Neahóra, with
its beach and tavernas.

Lake Kourná

Across the harbour from the Maritime Museum you'll see
the impressive buttressed dome of the **Giáli Tzamí** 🄳 (Shore
Mosque), the first mosque built by the Ottomans in 1645. Beyond
the mosque leads to the inner harbour, with the remains of large
Venetian **arsenália** (ship repair yards) – originally 17 lined the
water's edge. You can then continue out along the pier to the 19th-
century lighthouse at the harbour mouth.

The old quarters extend behind the harbour: narrow alleyways
with a mélange of Venetian and Ottoman buildings, a canvas of
faded terracotta and ochre stucco dressed with restaurant signs
or wares for sale. The shopping here is the most sophisticated on
Crete, a legacy of Haniá's days as a bohemian hangout in the 1960s.

Although the streets all seem to run together, there are
four recognised sections of the old town. **Tophanás** ('Cannon
Hall' in Turkish) behind the Naval Museum, was the Ottoman

administrative quarter. Theotokopoúlou, lined with a string of fine Venetian mansions and fashionable cafés, bounds it to the west. At the corner of Zambelíou and Móskhon stands the **Renieri Gate**, built in 1608.

Evraïkí, to the southeast, was the Jewish Quarter during Venetian times. Its small houses awash with pastel hues offer the most shopping and eating possibilities. A synagogue, **Etz Hayyim** Ⓔ, has been restored for visits (www.etz-hayyim-hania. org; Mon–Thurs 10am–4pm, Fri 10am–3pm; free, but a donation is expected), although all of Haniá Jews were deported by the Germans. **Kastélli**, east of the Shore Mosque, was the centre of the Venetian city – as the name suggests there was an older castle here, rendered obsolete when Haniá expanded during the 16th century. You'll see a Venetian arcade at the bottom of Agíou Márkou. Kastélli was also the site of Minoan, Greek and Roman Kydonia, the ancient town, partly exposed on Kanevárou.

The easternmost old quarter is **Splántzia**, characterised by whitewashed churches and cobbled alleyways. Platía 1821 forms the core of this neighbourhood, which has more authentic daily life than any other part of old Haniá.

The **Archaeological Museum** of Chania Ⓕ (www-amch-gr; Wed–Mon: April–Oct 8am–8pm; Nov–March 8.30am–3.30pm) has recently moved to a new location in an iconic building in the historic suburb of Chalepa. The collection spans all eras but is strongest on painted Minoan *larnakes* (clay coffins), Roman statuettes, and Hellenistic mosaics.

Nearby is the **Folklore Museum "Cretan House"** Ⓖ (www. giralio.gr; daily: April–Oct 9am–8pm; Nov–March 9am–5pm), tucked away in a tiny square alongside the Roman Catholic church of the Assumption, essentially an old house crammed with antiques and textiles; reproductions of old embroidery are for sale.

Skrydlóf 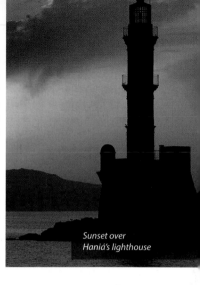 (Leather Street), with its mix of traditional goods and trashy souvenirs, heads off Halídon towards the **Agorá**, or covered market, one of Crete's shopping highlights.

WEST OF HANIÁ

As there are few good beaches near Haniá, many people stay in resorts to the west and simply travel in for the day. **Plataniás** is an excellent option with a lively atmosphere, as are **Agía Marína** and quieter **Geráni**.

Sunset over Haniá's lighthouse

Continuing west, **Máleme** is the furthest resort proper; after this, accommodation can be found only in private rooms or small local hotels. The town has a sad legacy, as it was the airfield here (still active) that German paratroopers first seized in 1941, signalling the start of the battle for Crete. Casualties were high for these pioneers, and the **German war cemetery** above the airfield holds the graves of more than 4,000 young men.

Beyond Máleme, the rugged peninsulas of **Rodopoú** and **Gramvoúsa**, jut out from the northern coast, offer plenty of excursions (best to the Goniá Monastery, and Ágios Ioánnis shrine, on Rodopoú, or the lagoon of Bálos on Gramvoúsa). They bracket the port town of **Kíssamos** 🐠 (aka Kastélli), unremarkable except for its superb **Archaeological Museum** (Tue–Sun 8am–3pm), strongest on Roman/ Hellenistic Kissamos, with a brilliant villa mosaic of 'The Seasons' upstairs. Beyond Kíssamos, the broad sandy beach at

Falásarna, complete with ancient town, and the beautiful lagoon at **Elafónisos** attract numerous day-trippers.

The route from Máleme to Paleóhora on the south coast provides a microcosm of what western Crete is all about. From the wide coastal plain, you climb, then drop, through small villages, the biggest – **Kándanos** – rebuilt after a wartime atrocity and sporting several unlocked, frescoed chapels. Your destination, **Paleohóra ㊷**, is a laid-back town with a crumbled Venetian fort and two beaches – Gialiskári (pebbles) and Pahiá Ammos (long and sandy) embracing it. A partly-pedestrianised main street offers every diversion after dark. This is also the end of the line for the south-coast ferries – you can head east towards Hóra Sfakíon.

A different road from Kándanos leads to **Soúgia ㊸**, an even more relaxed, smaller resort with a huge sand-and-pebble beach

Picturesque lane in Haniá's old town

(naturists throng the far end) and a variety of walking possibilities, including the scenic hour-plus hike west to **ancient Lissós** through a spectacular gorge.

> **Two islands**
>
> The two islands off Gramvoúsa Peninsula both take its name – Iméri (tame) and Ágria (wild) Gramvoúsa.

THE WHITE MOUNTAINS AND THE SAMARIÁ GORGE

The **White Mountains** ④④ (Lefká Óri), the island's highest range, with several peaks exceeding 2,000m (5,600ft), dominate western Crete. There are almost no villages on its south flank because the mountains rise so abruptly from the Libyan Sea. This is an unforgiving landscape, rugged and stunningly beautiful, with narrow valleys between limestone peaks that wear a mantle of snow until May. Yet these mountains host one of Crete's most impressive, popular and enjoyable excursions – the 16km (10-mile) walk down the famous **Samariá Gorge** ④⑤ (www.samaria.gr; May–mid-Oct daily 6am–4pm; entrances at Xylóskala and Agía Rouméli). Starting at an elevation of 1,240m (4,068ft), the gorge is the longest in Europe, swollen with meltwater during winter. Only during summer, when the torrent shrinks to a trickle, are people allowed to follow its path. Ancient cypress trees, rare orchids and soaring birds of prey are the overwhelming attractions.

Despite the strenuous nature of the trek – don't set out without sturdy footwear, a hat, sunscreen and a full water bottle – you'll share the narrow pathway with hundreds of other intrepid tourists, which adds to the camaraderie, but can spoil the atmosphere if you hoped for solitude. However early you start, you're unlikely to beat the crowds. Most people pay for an excursion that provides a bus ride to the head of the gorge at **Xylóskala** (wooden staircase) and boat transfer from Agía Rouméli, at the southern end, to Hóra Sfakión where you rejoin the bus. If you travel independently, you

Wild goats

The Samariá Gorge is one of the few places where you might catch a glimpse of the elusive Cretan wild goat known as the *agrími* or *krí-krí*. Built like an ibex, with long curving adult horns, it is sometimes spotted leaping between crags in the White Mountains.

can take a bus from Haniá to Omalós, just before Xylóskala, and then board a boat east to Hóra Sfakíon, or west to Soúgia or Paleohóra.

The National Park containing the gorge opens daily at 6am from May to mid-October; after 3pm the main section is closed. Park wardens sell you a ticket, to be surrendered at the other end to ensure that no one is left stranded in the gorge. The descent begins at Xylóskala, in fact a steeply descending path with wooden balustrades for much of the way. With wall-like **Mt Gíngilos** towering above, the stone path drops sharply away in a series of switchbacks, falling 1,000m (3,300ft) in the first 3km (2 miles).

The route becomes less steep once you reach the **Chapel of Ágios Nikólaos**, 4km (2.5 miles) in, where there is a picnic area. Springtime freshwater pools are inviting, but swimming is strictly forbidden. The abandoned village of **Samariá**, with its 14th-century **Church of Osía María** (Mary the Anointed of Egypt), marks the halfway point. People lived here until 1962; now there's only a warden's post and first-aid station. Beyond looms the gorge's narrowest, most memorable point, the **Siderespórtes** (Iron Gates), only 3.5m (11ft) wide but 300m (1,000ft) high. Beyond this, the gorge opens up as it approaches the sea and is much less striking. The final stretch is perhaps the most gruelling as you walk along the shadeless riverbed, but at **Agía Rouméli** ⓰ you'll be able to enjoy an extremely welcome drink or meal.

EXCURSION TO SANTORÍNI

Although Crete is interesting and varied, you may want to spend a day or two exploring a different Greek island. **Santoríni** (aka **Thíra**) is one of the most beautiful places in the world, and just a couple of hours by fast catamaran from Iráklio. Day trips are offered in every resort.

Arriving by sea allows gradual comprehension of the stunning topography unfolding before you, for Santoríni frames the largest submerged volcanic caldera on earth. A massive eruption of this volcano around 1500BC carried the whole interior of the island high into the atmosphere as ash, changing the climate of the earth for years afterwards. In place of land came water, surging in to fill the 11km (7-mile) -long void and causing massive tidal waves around the Aegean. What remains today is the outer rim of the original circular island. Sheer cliffs up to 300m (980ft) high bound the caldera, and a number of whitewashed settlements nestle along their crests.

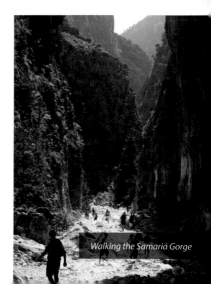

FIRÁ

The island capital is **Firá**, perched atop high cliffs in the centre of the long interior curve. Its buildings tumble towards the water below, giving stunning views. A narrow, cobbled trail of 587 steps leads from the town to the small port below, now the domain of

Walking the Samariá Gorge

a fleet of donkeys that wait to carry cruise-ship passengers into town. There is also a quicker cable car that whisks you up from sea level in a couple of minutes. Most commercial ferries arrive at the new port of **Athiniós** south along the coast.

Firá's narrow, traffic-free alleys make up a shopper's paradise; you can buy anything from a reproduction icon to a genuine Fabergé egg, designer jewellery of the finest quality and designer clothing by the most desirable names. Find a spot for a drink at sunset, which has to be one of the most spectacular on earth.

Among the boutiques and bars are three places of cultural interest. The **Museum of Prehistoric Thíra** (bit.ly/TheraMuseum; summer Wed–Mon 8.30am–3.30pm) and the **Archaeological Museum** (closed at the time of writing, check website before visiting; bit.ly/TheraArch) display pottery and other artefacts found on the island. The **Mégaron Gýzi Museum** (www.gyzi-megaron.gr; May–Oct Mon–Sat 10am–4pm), north of the cable-car station, is housed in a beautiful 17th-century fortified house. Most exciting of its varied collections are photographs showing island scenes from before the devastating 1956 earthquake – the last major one to strike Santoríni.

Santoríni's capital, Firá

ÍA

Firá is beautiful, but can get a little oppressive as visitors crowd the narrow streets. A little way northwest is a smaller town where the pace is a little less frantic. At **Ía** (often written Oia), set on the northern cliffs, the 1956 damage was more sensitively repaired; many homes are still built into the hillsides, and some have been converted into art galleries and shops selling crafts and souvenirs.

PÝRGOS, PROFÍTIS ILÍAS AND AKROTÍRI

Aside from the stunning views, Santoríni has many more delights, Including 12 villages to visit set among agricultural land. The fertile volcanic soil is blanketed by vines producing the renowned local wine, or plants producing tiny, sweet tomatoes. Near the island centre is **Pýrgos** village, with the remains of a Venetian fortress at its core. On a rocky summit to the south stands 17th-century **Profítis Ilías Monastery**. The monastery is only opened for morning or evening liturgy, but it is well worth coinciding with the priest to visit. Pride of place goes to a 15th-century icon of the prophet Elijah. It also has a museum, which conveys a flavour of monastic life. Unfortunately, the hilltop also bristles with antenna and military paraphernalia, meaning outside photographs are prohibited. On the east coast, **Kamári** and **Périssa** have beaches of fine black or red sand – another legacy of volcanic origins – which heat to a ferocious temperature in the summer sun.

In Santoríni's far south is one of the most important ancient sites in the Mediterranean. Near the modern village of **Akrotíri**, a complete city was discovered dating from before 2000BC (bit.ly/AkrotiriSite; summer Mon, Wed & Thurs 8.30am–3.30pm, Tues, Fri, Sat & Sun 8am–8pm). It was totally covered by several feet of ash during the eruption *c.*1500BC but, unlike at Pompeii in Italy, no human remains have been found, leading scientists to believe that the population managed to escape. Since 1967 the site has been painstakingly excavated to give a picture of daily life before the great eruption. A complex and sophisticated society is being unveiled, probably a colony of Minoan Crete, with organized urban planning, heating and sanitation.

Crete offers a wealth of opportunities
for beach activities

THINGS TO DO

SPORT

BEACH ACTIVITIES

Crete has hundreds of beaches. With everything from tiny coves to lengthy stretches, you can choose to spend your day with hundreds of others or have the sand all to yourself at a secluded spot. Beaches in the main resorts have well-organised watersports facilities with jet-skis, water-rides, kayaking and parasailing. The biggest are located around Agios Nikólaos, Liménas Hersónisou, Mália and Réthymno on the north coast. Head east for excellent windsurfing, especially Koureménos near Palékastro.

South-coast resorts tend to be more low-key; beaches are generally smaller, in discrete bays rather than on long stretches of shoreline. You'll find the most diverse range of beach activities at Mátala, Agía Galíni, Plakiás, Mýrtos and Paleohóra.

Váï, in the far northeastern corner, is considered the most exotic beach on Crete, and, like Elafónisos in the far southwest, gets extremely busy in summer. More remote beaches, where you'll find some solitude, are at the end of steep tracks which may or may not be paved.

WALKING AND HIKING

Walking in Crete is amply rewarded with small remote villages, hidden churches and a rural lifestyle to explore. Itineraries can range from short easy walks to steep mountain ascents; however, it's not advisable to head into the high peaks without good maps and a trekking guide. The best all-in-one title is Loraine Wilson's *The High Mountains of Crete* (Cicerone), with reliable route descriptions and sketch maps.

Hiking in southern Crete

The European long-distance E4 trail threads the island from Kíssamos to Káto Zákros, and full (or partial) traverses have become increasingly common. Gorge walks are also popular; the Samariá is the busiest and the longest. Others include the Imbros and Askífou Gorges near Samariá, the Rouvás Gorge near Záros on Mt Psilorítis, and the Hokhlahiés and Zákros canyons on the east coast. The peninsulas off the northwest coast offer dramatic and interesting walks, for example the trek to Agios Ioánnis chapel on Rodopoú. Akrotíri is not as rugged as Gramvoúsa and Rodopoú, but does have an excellent route between Agía Triáda and Katholikó monasteries. Other rewarding short itineraries can be found around Soúgia (southwest coast).

You'll find local agencies arranging organised hiking tours in many resorts, and plenty of overseas specialist companies offer organised hiking holidays on Crete.

CYCLING

Mountain biking and cycle touring are becoming increasingly popular. Remember, though, that Crete is extremely mountainous. In some resorts, especially in the west, local companies offer easy cycling tours, with a bus following behind to help you up the hills.

DIVING AND SNORKELLING

The waters around Crete, especially off the southwest coast, offer interesting diving and snorkelling opportunities for water-lovers with all levels of experience. Although the Mediterranean is overfished and its waters not warm enough to support colourful tropical fish, there are still numerous species to spot in the rocky shallows, including octopus that make their homes in crevices. The remains of many ancient sites lie just off the coast.

The Greek government is anxious to preserve submerged archeological treasures, so diving is strictly regulated and permitted only with a qualified dive company that oversee underwater activities.

If you have never tried scuba diving before, each dive centre is licensed by the government to offer training in addition to dive supervision for qualified divers. The basic qualification, an Open Water Certificate, normally takes five days to complete. Many centres also offer introductory sessions.

ENTERTAINMENT

Numerous fairs and festivals take place throughout the year. Local tourist offices will have details of what's happening during your stay on Crete. Each community celebrates its patron saint's day, when the saint's icon is usually paraded through the streets. After a solemn religious service, the rest of the day (or evening) is given over to revelry. These are the best

Learning to dive

If you are learning to dive, make sure you choose a dive centre affiliated with one of the major certifying bodies: PADI (the Professional Association of Diving Instructors), BSAC (British Sub-Aqua Club) and CMAS (Confédération Mondiale des Activités Subaquatiques) are the most common.

places to see traditional Cretan dances and live music, and to join in with local people having fun.

MUSIC AND DANCE

For many, Greek music and dance is inexorably linked to the film *Zorba the Greek*, with Anthony Quinn performing the *syrtáki*, an amalgam of several traditional dances, accompanied by the *bouzoúki*. Taverna owners' habit of playing this tune at high volume does a great disservice to the rich and venerable music tradition of Crete, where traditional instrumentalists and singers are held in high regard.

Musical rhythms throughout Greece are very different from the 'four beats to a bar' that characterises western music, and can be difficult for foreign would-be dancers to follow. Song lyrics, usually sung by men, refer not only to the hard life of shepherds,

ZORBA'S DANCE

The film *Zorba the Greek* brought international fame to author Nikos Kazantzakis' 1946 novel. Michael Cacoyannis, a Greek filmmaker of Cypriot origin, made the film in 1964 with Anthony Quinn in the leading role as Alexis Zorba. His famous *syrtáki* dance scene dismayed the islanders, as it's not a genuine Cretan dance. The indigenous *pendozáli* proved too difficult for the American actor to learn, so soundtrack composer Mikis Theodorakis came up with a simple but danceable melody in its place. The hordes of tourists who later came to Crete asked to see a dance that did not actually exist, but hoteliers and the music industry moved quickly to oblige them. *Syrtáki* is performed at today's 'Cretan evenings', and recordings of the catchy tune are available everywhere. But be aware it's not the traditional dance of Crete at all.

farmers and fishermen, but also touch on love (especially unrequited) – an element of sentimentality rarely expressed directly at other times.

Crete's main traditional musical instrument is the *lýra*, a three-stringed lap fiddle, played upright. It is usually accompanied by the *laoúto*, a long-necked, fretted development of the Arab *oud* (lute), and sometimes the *askomandoúra* (bagpipes with two chant-

A tradition of dance

ers but no drone). These instruments typically accompany *mantinádes*, sung rhyming couplets. Some of these have been passed down through generations of Cretans, but many are improvised on the spot. The men of the western Lefká Óri range sing sparsely accompanied songs, the *rizítika*, elegies for battles and heroic personages. The mountain men also have their distinctive, martial *pendozális* dance; in Réthymno and other coastal towns, the pan-Aegean *soústa* is common.

Chanting epic poetry is also a long-standing Cretan tradition. The 17th-century epic *Erotokritos*, written by Vitsentzos Kornaros in local dialect, is the most popular of these, having inspired many modern Greek poets, and has been set to music repeatedly.

Good places to see traditional music include the mid-summer festivals of the largest towns (see page 101). Throughout the island, larger hotels stage weekly 'Greek nights', or organise excursions to events at village tavernas. The music and dance is usually of a high standard, although surroundings are hardly authentic. More atmospheric is Tavern To Adespoto in Haniá at the corner of Sifáka and Melchisedek, which offers live music every evening from 7.30pm (www.adespotochania.gr). An intimate venue for all kinds of acoustic music (including Cretan) is the first-floor bar of the Pagopoieio, which also offers executive suites, on Platía Agíou Títou in central Iráklio (www.pagopoieion.gr).

In far eastern Crete, near Palékastro, another unlikely but wonderful acoustic stage is Maridatis (www.maridatis.gr), a musical taverna behind the eponymous cove, featuring named Greek performers every Friday and Saturday throughout the summer.

If you want to study music seriously, there's an excellent musical workshop centre in Houdétsi village, near Iráklio; see www.labyrinthmusic.gr for details. In summer they run open seminars and master classes on both Greek and foreign music. More casually, patronize the excellent Aerakis CD shop at Platia Korai 14 in Iráklio (www.aerakis.net), which specialises in local musicians.

SHOPPING

Shopping is one of the delights of a visit to Crete; souvenirs abound in all quality and price ranges. Most resort souvenir shops cater to mass-market tastes, but you can find locally produced goods, especially along the narrow streets of the old towns, providing hours of browsing. Marked prices can be flexible, particularly in tourist shops and at the beginning and end of the season.

TEXTILES

Sheep's wool and goat's hair have always been used to produce handwoven material (*yfandá*), clothing and interesting carpets or throw rugs. Today, machine-produced items far outnumber handmade pieces. Brighter colours often indicate synthetic dyes, whereas traditionally made items show the muted earthy colours of natural dyes. The price differential will also indicate which is which.

Dolphins and fish are popular themes, as are stylised images of Greek gods. You'll find particularly interesting ranges in Kritsá and Anógia, and also on the approach to the Dictaean Cave in Lasíthi and in shops

Souvenirs for sale in Iráklio

in Haniá. The only remaining traditional loom-weaver in Crete is Mihalis Manousakis, at his shop Roka (Zampelíou 61, tel: 28210 74736) located in Haniá's Venetian outer port. Top Hanas, nearby (Angélou 3; best to call Kostas for opening times; tel: 69787 03592) is a treasure-trove of antique Cretan textiles, but they don't come cheap and the owner admits he has to bulk up the stock with imported items.

If rugged textiles don't appeal, then you'll also find beautiful embroidered items such as cotton and linen tablecloths and napkins. Again the hand-embroidered pieces are the best and most expensive, but this skill is a dying art, so good examples are becoming harder to find. However, you will have plenty of everyday tablecloths to choose from in markets and the main tourist centres. The Centre of Traditional Folk Art and Culture (Skoufón 20, tel: 28210 92677) in Evraïki, Haniá sells a collection of remarkable modern embroidery.

Buying antiques

There are some excellent copies of museum pieces for sale. These will come complete with a certificate of authentication, which you may need to show to customs as you depart. If you want to buy a genuine antique (anything produced before 1821), you will need a permit to export it. Always consult an expert when you do this in order to avoid subsequent problems.

LEATHER GOODS

Leather remains extremely good value in Greece with bags, purses, luggage and belts found in abundance – try Skrydlóf Street in Haniá to begin comparing quality and prices.

Traditional leather sandals (flat soles with leather straps) are still sold in the streets of Réthymno and Haniá. There is also a traditional workshop at Kritsá, but nowadays modern mass-produced fashion shoes sadly seem to be displacing them. You can also purchase a pair of *stivánia*, Cretan shepherd's boots – almost knee-high black leather with thick soles. They are guaranteed to last decades and, judging by the number of well-worn pairs on feet in the hinterland, that certainly seems true. These are handmade to order, will take about a week to complete, and are accordingly expensive.

KNIVES AND ANTIQUES

Hand-forged Cretan knives are made by various knife-makers, especially in Réthymno and Haniá; stainless-steel blades are fitted to olive-wood, bone or horn handles, and are usually inscribed with an appropriate *mantináda* (rhyming couplet). One of the best shops in Haniá's traditional knife-making district (Maherádika) is O Armenis (www.armenis-knife-shop.business.site) at Sifáka 14, owned by Michail Pakhtikos. Just a few paces away at Sifáka 18 is Crete's best antique outlet, Tzangarakis (www.tsangarakis.com), specialising in watches, jewellery and accessories.

CLOTHING

In terms of warm-weather fashions, you should be able to buy everything you need in Crete, so don't worry if you can't find appropriate summer clothes or swimwear at home before you leave. Early and late in the season you can buy good-quality cotton sweaters to guard against evening chill.

Stores in the big towns – including chain outlets like Zara and Benetton – stock major designer labels. Prices can be high by EU standards; summer sales run from late July.

EDIBLES

Olives and olive oil are obvious souvenir choices; the quality of both is considered among the best in Greece. Particularly good are extra virgin cold-pressed oils from Sitía, Toploú and Agía Triáda.

Honey is also one of the prime staples of the Cretan diet; wild herbs and flowers on the hills impart a wonderful flavour.

A variety of herbs are collected and dried for you to take home and use in your cooking. Basil, thyme and oregano are the most common, though you can also

Olives ripening on the tree

buy mixed sachets. Dittany *(díktamos)* herb has been used to make tea on the island for centuries; sage *(faskomiliá)* and mountain ironwort *(malotíra)* are also popular tea-bases.

ART AND ICONS

Artists flocked to Haniá from the early 1960s onwards, and this has left a legacy in the quality of work on sale here (and to a lesser extent across Crete). There are several galleries displaying work by local and international artists in the narrow alleyways of the Evraïkí quarter. A more Greek art form is the icon or religious portrait, usually of a saint or apostle, and lie at the heart of Byzantine or Orthodox worship as they form a focus for prayer. For centuries, icons were popular souvenirs of the European Grand Tour or religious pilgrimage. However, modern production methods using gaudy synthetic colours saw them lose favour. In recent years there has been a rebirth in icon-painting using traditional methods, both for church renovations and for commercial sale. This time-consuming work is exquisite and correspondingly expensive. Most monasteries on Crete create certified copies of their most celebrated icons, and you can also find them in jewellery shops in the towns.

JEWELLERY

Both gold and silver are sold by weight, with relatively little extra cost for workmanship, so they represent good value for money. Ancient Minoan patterns are common with necklaces, bracelets and rings in matching sets. You can also find items featuring precious and semi-precious stones. The House of Amber, Kondyláki 13, Evraïkí district, Haniá, specialises in amber 'worry beads' *(kombológia)*. However, you don't need a large budget to buy trinkets; popular street jewellery uses leather, semi-precious stones and crystals.

POTTERY AND CERAMICS

It's not surprising – given the importance of pottery throughout Crete's history – that it is still a significant industry. Pieces come as small as a ring holder to huge garden pieces. Both unglazed and glazed styles are available; most notable of these is the bright-blue glaze of Haniá ceramics. Traditional designs abound, including marine themes, Minoan designs and Classical Greek imagery. Modern abstract pieces can also be found, particularly in Haniá, where avant-garde potters stock galleries. At Margarítes you can watch the potters at work and buy from their workshops.

OLIVE-WOOD ITEMS

Annual prunings and heftier trunk wood are fashioned into a myriad of useful or decorative items: cutting boards, cooking utensils,

Local ceramics for sale in Haniá

napkin rings, candle holders. Cutting boards should ideally be one piece and not made of glued-together sections. Large pieces require long seasoning and are hard to work, thus don't come cheaply. One particular workshop to recommend, off the beaten track, is Nikos Vostakis (tel: 28330 41061) in Vyzári village off the Amári valley.

CHILDREN'S CRETE

Crete isn't all about museums and ancient sites – there's also lots of fun to be had for younger members of the family. Greek society is very family-oriented, and children will be very welcome at tavernas and cafés.

Beach activities are well-organised on the northern coast, with all types of watersports and rides. The best sandy beaches are at Mália, Réthymno, Georgioúpoli and Váï. South-coast resorts such as Plakiás, Paleohóra and Mátala have good beaches and plenty of snorkelling opportunities for older children. Waterparks near Haniá (Limnoupolis; www.limnoupolis.gr), Iráklio (www.watercity.gr) and Liménas Hersonísou (www.acquaplus.gr) will keep them occupied for hours.

A horse-and-carriage ride through the streets of Haniá is a great treat and gives young children a good vantage point. Trips along the coast in colourful *caïques* offer the chance to enjoy a cooling breeze and an alternative view of the island. Castles such as the Koúles in Iráklio, Réthymno's Fortezza and Frangokástello allow imaginations to run wild.

The rural lifestyle of the interior – watching goats filing past, or donkeys working hard for their owners – will delight urban children. Older children should also see gorge walks as exciting adventures. If you want to spend some time apart from your kids, many larger hotels have children's clubs and crêches for toddlers.

CALENDAR OF FESTIVALS

Each Cretan community celebrates its own saint's day (often more than one), there are too many such celebrations, called *panigýria*, to list here. Below are the major events occurring across the island.

6 January: *Theofánia* (Epiphany). Youths dive for a crucifix thrown into harbours.

February/March: Street carnivals with floats and masquers in Réthymno and Iráklio on the two weekends before Lent.

March/May: Easter. *Epitáfios* processions on Good Friday; effigy of Judas burned on Saturday; in churches the sacred flame passes to worshippers' candles Saturday at midnight; on Sunday a lamb is barbecued for feasts.

23 April: Ágios Geórgios (St George), patron saint of shepherds; sheep-shearing festival in Así Goniá.

20–27 May: Battle of Crete commemorated at Máleme and Haniá.

23–24 June: St John the Baptist/Midsummer's Eve, celebrated with bonfires which are leapt over.

Late June: Casa dei Mezzo Music Festival (www.casadeimezzo.com). Classical chamber concert series.

July: Renaissance Festival of dramatic and musical performances held at Réthymno.

July–August: Kornaria Cultural Festival in Sitía.

July–September: Iráklio festival, with theatrical and music events.

15 August: *Kímisi tís Panagías* (Dormition of the Virgin). Celebrated throughout Crete, at churches dedicated to the Virgin.

25 August: Ágios Títos (St Titus, patron saint of Crete). Procession in Iráklio.

29 August: Ágios Ioánnis (John the Baptist). Pilgrimage on foot (4-hr round trip) to Ágios Ioánnis chapel on the Rodopoú Peninsula.

28 October: *Óhi* Day. Celebrates Greek defiance of Italians in World War II.

7–9 November: Commemoration of the Arkádi Monastery explosion with a fireworks display.

FOOD AND DRINK

Greek food has always incorporated local and seasonal ingredients at the peak of their flavour and freshness, served raw or cooked simply – grilled, flash-fried or slow-baked. Since Crete was settled several millennia ago, its people have relied on staples like olive oil, fragrant herbs, wild greens, seafood, lamb or goat meat, and an abundance of fresh garden vegetables, fruit, pulses and nuts. Combine these with more recent Venetian and Ottoman influences, and you have an interesting cuisine. The island shares many recipes with the Greek mainland, but it also has numerous ingredients and dishes found nowhere else.

Today, the traditional Cretan diet is considered to be one of the healthiest in the world, and it is well worth following locals to the better eateries to try it.

WHERE TO EAT

Crete has a range of eateries specialising in certain types of food and drink. Although the boundaries between them are blurring, the following explains what you can expect to find.

A *psistaría* offers charcoal-grilled meat dishes, plus a limited selection of salads and meze (*mezédes*). The *tavérna* is a more elaborate eatery, often family run, offering pre-cooked, steam-tray dishes known as *mageireftá*, as well as a few grills and bulk wine. A *psárotaverna* specialises in fish and seafood.

An *ouzerí* purveys not just that quintessentially Greek alcoholic drink, but also the meze dishes that complement it – *oúzo* is never drunk on an empty stomach. Octopus, olives, a piece of cheese or a platter of small fried fish are traditional accompaniments, but there will be various other platters to choose from. A *mezedopolío* is a more elaborate *ouzerí* where food takes precedence.

The *kafeníon* is the Greek coffee shop, traditionally a men-only domain, and still so in the inland villages. Usually very plainly decorated with old tables and chairs, they are often the venues for political debate and serious backgammon games.

WHEN TO EAT

Tavernas in resort areas may offer a full English breakfast as well as lunch and dinner or Sunday roast. Typically Greeks don't eat breakfast – a coffee and *friganiés* (melba toast) or a baked pastry is about as much as they'll indulge in. Lunch is eaten between 2.30 and 4pm, followed by a siesta before work begins again at 5.30pm. Dinner is eaten late, usually from 9.30pm onwards, and some establishments take last orders as late as midnight. You'll more often than not find tavernas closed on Sunday evenings and part or all of Monday.

WHAT TO EAT

You will usually be given an extensive menu; items currently available will have a price pencilled in beside them. But your waiter is the most reliable guide to what's available that day; menus can be used as guides to check that the taverna is within your budget, especially for typically pricey items like meat or fish. All restaurants render a cover charge. This includes a serving of bread

Al fresco lunch

A selection of appetising meze

and is usually no more than €1 per person – if you can, try *pax-imádia* (the traditional Cretan dry bread) or *dákos* (barley rusks), the latter often the basis of a popular salad (called *koukouvágia* in Réthymno district).

Appetisers

Carefully selected appetisers (meze, or *mezédes)* can constitute a full meal on Crete. Shared by the whole table, they're a fun and relaxing way to eat.

The most common meze are *tzatzíki*, a yoghurt dip flavoured with garlic, cucumber and mint; *dolmádes*, vine leaves stuffed with rice and vegetables – rarely mince – which can be served hot (with *avgolémono* sauce, made of eggs and lemon) or cold (with yoghurt); *taramosaláta*, cod-roe paste blended with breadcrumbs, olive oil and lemon juice; *gígandes*, large beans in tomato sauce; *keftedákia*, small meatballs flavoured with spices; *kalamarákia*, deep-fried squid; *plevrótous*, oyster mushrooms and *tyrokafterí*, a spicy cheese dip.

Saganáki is yellow cheese coated in breadcrumbs and then fried, while *féta psití* is feta cheese wrapped in foil with garlic and herbs and baked. *Kalitsoúnia* are little turnovers stuffed with greens or soft cheese, the latter often served with honey.

Cretan specialities include *volví skordaláta* (wild pickled narcissus bulbs with garlic), *marathópitta* (fried fennel pie), *apáki* (lean cured pork) and *sýnglino* (a fattier cured pork). Wild greens like *stífnos*, *stamnagáthi* (spiny chicory, often paired with meat) and *askolýmbri* (golden thistle) are especially popular. Greek salad or *horiátiki saláta* (literally 'village salad') consists of tomato, cucumber, onion, green peppers and olives topped with feta cheese. Cruets of olive oil and wine vinegar to dress it are found with other condiments on the table.

Soups are winter staples, but availability is more limited in summer. *Psarósoupa* (fish soup) is a standard on many seafood restaurant menus. *Fakés* (lentil), *revýthia* (chickpea) or *fasoláda* (bean) soups are excellent meatless options.

Fish and seafood

At fish tavernas, the day's catch is displayed on ice inside a chilled case for you to make your choice. It will be weighed, uncleaned, before cooking – check prices as seafood is almost always a relatively expensive option. If the seafood is frozen or farmed (likely from June to September), this must be stated on the menu – though often only in the Greek language column, or simply with an asterisk.

Larger fish is usually grilled or baked, and smaller fish fried; all are served with fresh lemon wedges or *ladolémono* (olive oil with lemon juice). The most common species of fish are *barboúni* (red mullet), *xifías* (swordfish), *koliós* (chub mackerel) and various breams. More elaborate seafood dishes include *ktapódi krasáto* (octopus stewed in a red wine and tomato sauce); *soupiá* (cuttlefish served with spinach rice); or *garídes saganáki* (prawns in a cheese sauce).

Meat main courses

Meaty takeaway snacks include *gýros* (thin pork slices cut from a vertical skewer and served with garnish and *tzatzíki* in pitta bread), or *souvláki* (small chunks of meat cooked on a skewer). Sit-down barbecued dishes include whole chickens, *loukánika* (sausages – the best being from Sfakiá district), sides of lamb or *soúvla* (rotisseried pork), all cooked to melting perfection. *Brizóla* – pork or veal – is a basic cutlet; lamb or goat chops, however, are *païdákia*. Roasted or barbecued lamb is the traditional post-Easter fare. Boiled goat *(gída vrastí)* is also a very popular village dish, often served with a side of *gamopílafo* (sticky white rice).

Stews include *kléftiko*, (braised lamb with tomatoes), *stifádo* (braised beef with onions) and *giouvétsi* (meat baked with lozenge-shaped *kritharáki* pasta) – each comes in a small clay pot that keeps the contents piping hot. *Tsigaristó* is a less elaborate stir-fry of lamb or goat chunks with vegetables.

SNAIL DELICACIES

Snails (*hokhlí*) from Crete are much prized throughout Greece. They are eaten fresh only during the warmer months, when they are dormant, or immediately after rain when they emerge, but are also served from frozen at Lent. *Hokhlí* are prepared in reputedly 40 different ways, including: scalded in salted water; stewed with potatoes and courgettes; fried in rosemary, garlic and oil; or, best of all, cooked with tomatoes, potatoes and thyme, in a dish called *egíni*.

Greece's most famous slow-cooked oven dish is *mousakás* – successive layers of aubergine (eggplant), potato slices and minced lamb topped with a layer of béchamel and seasoned with nutmeg; good restaurants make a fresh batch daily. *Pastítsio* is another layered oven-baked dish of macaroni, meat and cheese sauce.

For a hot meatless dish, *gemistá* are tomatoes, courgettes or peppers stuffed with herb-flavoured rice (though meat stock may be used). Alternatively *melitzánes imám* (eggplant baked richly with tomato, garlic and oil) is reliably vegetarian, as is *briám* or *tourloú* (ratatouille).

Fried seafood platter

Cheeses

Most Cretan cheeses are made from cow's, ewe's or goat's milk, or often blends of two of them. The best-known cheese is *féta*, featuring in every Greek salad or served alone garnished with olive oil and oregano. *Graviéra* and *kefalotýri* are the most common hard-grating cheeses, varying in sharpness; there are also many sweet soft cheeses such as *manoúri* and *anthótyro*. *Stáka* is clotted cream made from goat's milk.

Dessert

Most tavernas bring a plate of fresh seasonal fruit as a finale to your meal; for something more substantial, a *zaharoplastío* (cake shop) dishes out some decadent sweets, one of the more enduring legacies of the Ottomans: *baklavás*, layers of honey-soaked flaky pastry with walnuts; *kataïfi*, 'shredded wheat' filled with chopped almonds and honey; *galaktoboúreko*, custard pie; or *ravaní*, honey-soaked sponge cake. If you prefer dairy desserts, try yoghurt with local honey, or *ryzógalo*, cold rice pudding at a *galaktopolío*.

WHAT TO DRINK

Greek winemaking goes back over three millennia; quality has risen dramatically in recent decades. But owing to limited export – many wineries produce under 20,000 bottles annually – you're unlikely to have heard of even the best labels. Cretan wine in particular was celebrated throughout antiquity, only losing favour in relatively modern times.

Red, white or rosé are offered in full, half or quarter-litre measures, either in colourful aluminium vessels *(katroútza)* or in glass flagons. It is also available in bulk – *hýma* or *varelísio*. Quality varies considerably across the island; if in doubt, order a quarter-litre to start with as a test, and a can of soda to dilute it.

Oúzo is taken as an aperitif with ice and water; a compound in its anise flavouring makes the mix turn harmlessly cloudy. Cretans favour their own spirit *rakí*, distilled like *oúzo* from grape pressings, but unflavoured. Alcohol strength of either ranges from 40–50 percent.

> ### Favourite fruits
>
> Fruit platters after meals typically feature watermelon or Persian melon in summer; grapes or pears in autumn; sliced apples with cinnamon much of the year; and citrus or maybe even some strawberries in early spring. Greece imports just a few temperate fruits from Italy or Spain and relatively little tropical fruit, so this is pretty much the full repertoire.

It is the least expensive tipple on the island, often cheaper than bottled water; many tavernas offer a small *karafáki* (tumbler) of it on the house at the conclusion of the meal.

Nearly a dozen beers are produced in Greece, local labels include Fix, Vergina (reckoned to be the best two options), Alfa and Mythos. The Cretan Brewery near Chania makes Charma beers, which are unpasteurized and unfiltered.

A local favourite: raki

Non-alcoholic drinks

Hot coffee is served *ellínikós* or 'Greek' style, served in small cups. It will automatically arrive *glykós* (sweet) unless you order *métrios* (medium) or *skétos* (without sugar). Don't drink right to the bottom as that's where the grounds settle. Instant coffee *(nes)* has made big inroads in Greece; more appetising is *frappé*, cold instant coffee, whipped up in a blender with evaporated milk, rather like a coffee milkshake.

Soft drinks come in all the international varieties. Juices are usually from cartons rather than freshly squeezed. One of the most refreshing drinks is Cretan mineral water, fresh from mountain springs.

Dittany (*díktamo* or *érondas*) herb is sold across Crete. It is used to make an infusion claimed to have beneficial effects on a host of ailments. You won't find it on many restaurant menus, but you may be offered it if invited to a Cretan home.

TO HELP YOU ORDER

Could we have a table? **Boroúme na éhoume éna trapézi?**
Could we order, please? **Na parangiloúme, parakaló?**
a half litre **misó kiló**
I'm a vegetarian **Íme hortofágos**
Bon appetite **Kalí órexi**
Cheers! **Giámas!**
The bill, please **To logariazmó, parakaló**

MENU READER

arní lamb	**oktapódi** octopus
avgá eggs	**orektiká** starters
barboúni red mullet	**pagotó** ice cream
boútero butter	**(pagoméno) neró** (chilled) water
býra beer	
domátes tomatoes	**piperiés** peppers
eliés olives	**psári** fish
fasolákia runner beans	**psitó** roasted
froúta fruit	**psomí** bread
gala milk	**revýthia** chickpeas
garídes small shrimp	**rýzi** rice
gemistá stuffed	**saláta** salad
hirinó pork	**sídi** vinegar
hórta boiled greens	**soúpa** soup
katsíki goat	**spanáki** spinach
kotópoulo chicken	**sta kárvouna** grilled
kounélli rabbit	**sto foúrno** baked
krasí wine	**thalassiná** seafood
kréas meat	**tiganitó** fried
lahaniká vegetables	**tyrí** cheese
melitzánes aubergines	**xifías** swordfish
moskhári beef	**záhari** sugar

WHERE TO EAT

The following price ranges reflect the average cost of a two-course meal (per person) and a beer or share of bottled wine or *raki*. Except where indicated, reservations are rarely necessary (or even possible) – one waits, or an extra table may be fitted in. Unless indicated otherwise, all establishments accept card payment.

€€€€	over 33 euros
€€€	24–33 euros
€€	15–24 euros
€	under 15 euros

IRÁKLIO AND CENTRAL CRETE

Alekos €€ *Behind Agía Pelagía church, Vóri, tel: 28920 91094*. After visiting Phaistos and Agía Triáda, head for this secluded village taverna for a historic taste of Crete. The setting – a courtyard with tables and cushioned bench seating, and interior with a fireplace – is matched by the food: hearty portions of deftly executed recipes. A wood-burning oven bakes goat or kid dishes (ordered in advance). Daily lunch and dinner. Cash only.

Giakoumis € *Fotíou Theodosáki 5-8, Iráklio, tel: 28102 84039*. Popular classic market taverna specialising in succulent lamb chops, crispy potatoes, seasonal salads and equally good rosé or white bulk wine. Mon–Sat lunch and dinner. Cash only.

Ippokambos €€ *Sofoklí Venizélou 3, Iráklio, tel: 28102 80240*. Highly regarded *ouzerí* by the Venetian harbour. Excellent meze (including snails), reasonably priced fish and seafood, winning service. It gets busy, so go early; no reservations. April–Nov Tues–Sun lunch and dinner. Cash only.

Karnagio €€ *Dodekanisou 16, Nea Alikarnassos, Iráklio, tel: 28102 80090*. A local favourite, excellent for seafood like fish *mousaká* or shrimp *dakas*, plus rich risotto. The house wine is also excellent. Daily lunch and dinner. Credit cards accepted.

Kirkor € *Lion (Morosíni) Fountain Square, Iráklio, tel: 28102 42705.* Armenian-run stall with outdoor tables opposite the fountain, serving succulent *bougátsa* (custard pastry), *tyrópittes* (cheese pies) and good coffees since 1922. Daily from dawn until evening.

Paradosiako €€ *Vourváhon 9, Iráklio, tel: 28103 42927.* Secluded, no-nonsense taverna with courtyard seating and quirky interior; grills, meze and a few freshly prepared dishes of the day are the stock in trade. Mon–Sat 2pm–midnight. Cash only.

Spyros Taverna €€ *Pano Gouves, Gouves, tel: 69744 20937.* A traditional Greek taverna serving up tasty food in a cosy, inviting interior, reasonable prices, and a bonus pick-up and return taxi-drive to hotel. Daily 12.30pm–12.45am.

Vegera € *Zaros, Iráklio, tel: 28940 31730.* A renowned vegetarian restaurant with some meat options. The meal unfolds like this: your party gets a pitcher of cool water, then come salads, a plate of assorted cheeses and olives, several home-cooked local dishes, and finally: pastries and a shot of punchy *raki*. All ingredients are organic and mostly seasonal. Definitely worth a visit. Mon–Sat 8am–4pm, 7pm–11pm.

Votomos €€ *Near Lake Vótomos, Záros, tel: 69748 67233.* Trout specialists, relying on their own fish farm, though there are also lamb and chicken dishes. The setting, in the Psilorítis foothills, is idyllic, and it's a popular spot. April–Oct daily for lunch and dinner, winter weekends only.

ÁGIOS NIKÓLAOS AND THE EAST

Angistri €€ *Angathiás village centre, near Palékastro, tel: 28430 61598.* Some of the cheapest and freshest fish in the region, straight from Nikolas' boat. His son and daughter grill and serve, respectively. A few cooked dishes as well, plus superb views from the terrace by day. Daily 5pm–1am.

Avli Taverna €€ *Príngipa Georgíou 12, Ágios Nikólaos, tel: 28410 82479.* All the usual *ouzerí* standards, as well as desserts like lemon mousse. Polite service and a vine-shaded courtyard (*avlí* in Greek). The big plus is wine from their own vineyard in the Sitía mountains. Daily April–Oct Mon–Sat noon–1am, Sun until midnight. Cash only.

Faros €€ *Aktí Papá Nikolaou Pangálou 5, Kitroplatía cove, Ágios Nikólaos, tel: 28410 83168*. Family-run taverna located on Kitroplatia Beach right in the middle of town. Good grilled fish dishes and usual Greek staples such as *mousaká, dolmádes, gýros* and *tyrópittes* washed down with retsina and local wine. Daily noon–midnight.

Gioma Meze €€ *Dionisou Solomou 12, Ágios Nikólaos*, www.giomameze. com. Delightful fish and meze restaurant overlooking the harbour. Try their mushroom stew as an appetiser, shrimp tartare with creamed avocado or braised lamb shank. Daily noon–midnight.

Haroupia (The Carob Tree) €€ *Pláka, opposite Spinalónga, tel: 28410 42510*. Something of an oddity in a seafood-mad resort, this very competent, Greek-patronised *ouzerí* straddling the through-road does simpler, sustaining fare – *apáki*, mushrooms, *dolmádes* and *rakí*. Occasional live music. Daily 8am–midnight. Cash only.

Káto Zákros Bay €€ *Waterfront, Káto Zákros, tel: 28430 26687*. Tellingly, this taverna at one of eastern Crete's remotest bays gets the most local clientele, for the home-grown vegetables and poultry, fair prices and decent quality. April–Oct, open all day. Cash only.

Kohylia €€ *East quay, Mókhlos, tel: 28430 94432*. A reliable choice amongst several establishments here, also the oldest (founded 1902). Expect fresh artichokes in spring, stews, and daily casseroles like stuffed vegetables or *mousakás*. Feb–Nov, lunch and dinner.

Levante €€ *Stratigoú Samaíl 38, Ierápetra*, www.levante-taverna.gr. The most reliable of the string of tavernas behind the seafront. Castle views are matched by homely dishes like milk-based *xýgalo*, stuffed cabbage leaves, *papoutsáki* and *omathiés* (rice-and-offal sausage). Open all year.

Zygos €€ *Kaló Horió centre, near Istron, tel: 6973005012*. Whole goats roasting on spits out front announce this traditional taverna, with the management sourcing ingredients from their own farm. It can get raucous in high season, but Dimítris is a great host. Daily, 11am–midnight.

RÉTHYMNO, HANIÁ, THE SOUTHWEST

Anchorage €€ *Main access road, Soúgia, tel: 28230 51487*. Forego sea views in favour of a vine-shaded courtyard and decent renditions of *angináres me koukiá* (artichoke hearts with broad beans), wild *hórta*, stewed rabbit and *tsigaristó*. The house wine here is particularly good. Daily Easter–Oct, noon–11pm. Cash only.

Dounias €€ *Main access road, Drakona,* www.ntounias.gr. A picturesque family-owned small restaurant off the beaten track at the foot of the White Mountains. The Dounias family runs their own farm, produces olive oil and uses only local ingredients in their traditional, rustic dishes. Slow food and slow service, but a unique dining experience overall. Wed–Sun 11am–6pm.

Ta Chalkina €€ *Aktí Tombazi 29–30, old harbour, Haniá,* www.chalkina.com. Tucked between the tourist traps of the two Venetian ports is this *rakádiko*, well attended for titbits like eggplant roulade, *marathópita* (fennel pie) and *apáki*. Oddly, their bulk wine is preferable to their *raki*. Daily noon–1am. Cash only.

Ifigeneia €€ *Angouselianá, west outskirts, 10km (6 miles) from Spíli or Plakiás, tel: 28320 51362*. A shrine of traditional Cretan culinary delicacies like *volví skordaláta* (pickled wild hyacinth bulbs), *stamnagáthi, apáki* and boiled goat with *gamopílafo* (white sticky rice). Wed–Mon 2pm–midnight. Reservations recommended.

Ouzythino €€ *Akti Kanari 7, Nea Chora, Haniá, tel: 69731 79700*. This is a popular taverna, thanks to the generous helpings of marinated anchovies, Sfakian sausages, courgette patties and cheese-stuffed peppers. Daily lunch and dinner. Cash only.

Rakodikeio €€ *Vernádou 7, opposite Nerantzés Mosque, Réthymno, tel: 28310 54437*. This exquisite little *ouzerí* offers creatively tweaked dishes like pork fried with saffron and ouzo. Mid-summer for dinner only, otherwise 2pm until very late. Cash only.

Rembetiko Taverna €€ *Sougia seafront*, www.rembetiko-taverna-business. site. At this lovely taverna right on the seafront of Sougia, you can dine in the sheltered courtyard on traditional Cretan staples such as lamb shank, rabbit or *dolmádes*. Daily noon–12.30am.

Strata €€ *Portou 54, Haniá*, www.strata-restaurant.business.site. A popular tavern in Hania's Venetian harbour, usually packed as the food is really good. Huge portions, salads are conspicuously big, so don't order too much. Excellent service and friendly atmosphere. Occasional concerts in the evening. Daily noon–10.30pm.

Strofi tis Yefsis € *Vyzári, Amári Valley, Akrotíri Peninsula; tel: 28330 41258*. An excellent lunch stop while touring the valley. Expect simple fare like rabbit, snails and chips cut as medallions, washed down by their own strong wine. Open all year, as and when. Cash only.

Tamam €€€€ *Zambeliou 49, Evraïkí district, Haniá*, www.tamamrestaurant. com. This former *hamam* built in 1645 conceals one of the best, most atmospheric restaurants in town. The fare is Cretan, plus Mediterranean/Middle Eastern specialities like Iranian pilaf and lots for vegetarians. Daily Mon–Sat noon–12.30am, Sun until midnight.

The Third Eye €€ *50m inland from west beach, south end, Paleohóra*, www. thirdeye-paleochora.com. A remarkable vegetarian restaurant with an extensive and imaginative Asian/Indian menu, plus a tantalising range of desserts. Breakfast also offered. Occasional concerts by night. Daily lunch and dinner. Cash only.

Zorbas € *Behind the giant eucalyptus, near bus stop, Stavrós, Akrotíri peninsula; tel: 2821 039402*. Generally, you should run a mile from tavernas so-named, but this one's the real deal – the most locally attended of several on this sandy cove, where the disastrous log-transport scene of *Zorba the Greek* was filmed. There's a good range of seafood, cheeses, lamb dishes and vegetable casseroles in big portions. Open all year. Cash only.

TRAVEL ESSENTIALS

PRACTICAL INFORMATION

A

ACCOMMODATION (See also Recommended hotels, page 136)

Hotels: Many resort hotels have contracts with tour operators. If travelling between mid-July and early September, always make a firm reservation before arrival to avoid disappointment. October prices are generally much lower than at peak season. Most resort hotels close from November to March inclusive, although some hotels in the larger northern coastal towns stay open all year.

Rooms, apartments and studios: Except at the top end of the quality scale, the vast majority of accommodation in Crete is in modern, purpose-built blocks of rooms, studios or apartments, usually family-owned and run, simply furnished, yet almost always immaculately clean. The fancier places may be small complexes built around a pool and a small bar or restaurant. Apartments and studios will have some form of cooking facilities, larger apartments may have up to three bedrooms, making them ideal for families.

In the UK, some of the best agencies specialising in packages for high-quality self-catering premises, villas and hotels include Pure Crete (www.purecrete.com), Sunvil (www.sunvil.co.uk), The Villa Collection (www.gicthevillacollection.com) and Cachet Travel (www.cachet-travel.co.uk).

> I'd like a single/double room with bath/shower **Tha íthela éna monóklino/díklino me bánio/dous**
> How much (does it cost)? **Póso káni?**

AIRPORTS

International, charter and domestic flights to Crete serve the airports at **Iráklio** (Heraklion; HER), for central and eastern resorts, and **Haniá** (CHQ) for the western part of the island. The airport at **Sitía** (JSH), in the far east, only has domestic flights for now; unfortunately an ambitious expansion of the terminal to accept international ones has stalled for lack of funds.

Iráklio International Airport (aka Heraklion or "Nikos Kazantzakis"; bit.ly/HeraklionAirport) is the biggest of all three, and can be horribly crowded at times. There's a bus servicing the 5km (3 miles) route to and from Platía Eleftherías in the centre of town until late at night. There is also a bus service from Haniá airport (bit.ly/ChaniaAirport) the 14km (8.5 miles) to the city, but it's so infrequent (5–8 daily) that most arrivals take taxis – also the only option at Sitía, barring a 1.2km (0.7-miles) downhill walk into town.

B

BICYCLE AND SCOOTER HIRE

Bicycle hire: The mountains make long-distance cycling tough work, but in most resorts, you can hire mountain bikes and they'll usually offer good advice on where to explore. Some local travel agents also offer easy bike tours, with a bus to take you up the hills and carry your gear.

Scooter hire: Hiring a motorbike is inexpensive – roughly €33 per day in high season for a 50cc machine, or slightly more for a larger engine size. It is illegal to ride a bike of any size without a motorcycle licence – but many hire agencies ignore this legislation. Note that if you ride a motorbike without the right licence, any insurance you have will be void, which could create grave difficulties if you are involved in an accident. Quad bikes, also widely available, are legal to drive with Class B car licenses. Blue Sea, Kosmá Zótou 5-7 (Ikostipémptis Avgoústou) is a reliable Iráklio company that hires scooters and motorbikes (tel: 28102 41097; www.bluesearentals.com).

What's the hire charge for a full day? **Póso kostízi giá mía méra?**

BUDGETING FOR YOUR TRIP

Crete offers good value for money, especially compared to most other parts of Greece. Here are some approximate prices to help you to plan your budget.

Flight from Athens to Iráklio (one way): €50–180 by season

Adult ferry ticket from Athens: €46/180 (basic seating/in cabin)

High-season room in mid-range hotel: €75–125 per night

Meal in mid-range taverna per person: €15–20

Taxi fare from airport to Haniá: €25

Entrance fee for museums/sites: €2–6

Car hire (prebooked): small car for two weeks: €350

C

CAMPING

There are camp sites near most major towns and resorts, but these get extremely busy in July and August, and are aimed mainly at camper vans. Wild camping is officially prohibited, but communities of free campers form at 'alternative' havens like Soúgia, Léndas, Falássarna and on the offshore islet of Gávdos.

CAR HIRE

The best car hire rates (under €30 per day) apply to periods of four days or more, with unlimited mileage. Distances on Crete can be considerable, so limited mileage tariffs aren't cost effective. One-way rentals (pick up at one airport, drop off at another) incur surcharges of €35–70.

Reserving before you arrive through an international hire company can be useful, as in peak season demand will be high. Some of the best consolidator websites include www.auto-europe.co.uk; www.carrentals.co.uk; www.rentalcars.com, who also have a downloadable app; and www.rentalcargroup.com. **Alianthos** (tel: 28320 31851; www.alianthos-group.com) is an excellent local operator, with offices at airports and major resorts.

You will need a credit card for a damages deposit and a full national licence (held for at least one year) from your country of residence. Non-

EU licence holders must, by Greek law, also have an International Driving Permit except US and UK drivers, where just their national photo driving licence is required. If you fail to provide this, many agencies will refuse to release the car, and if you are caught by the police without it, fines can range upwards of €1000.

Depending on the model and the hire company, the minimum age for hiring a car varies from 21 to 25. Third-party liability insurance and Collision Damage Waiver is usually included in the stated rate, but there is usually a large excess (typically €400–750) before CDW takes effect. One reputable outfit selling such policies is Insurance4CarHire (www. insurance4carhire.com).

CLIMATE

Crete has an average of 320 sunny days per year. Winters are mild, although it can suddenly become cold and wet for short spells. In general, the south coast is hotter, drier and less windy than the north. About 70 percent of the annual rainfall falls between December and March. These are the approximate monthly average temperatures in Iráklio:

	J	F	M	A	M	J	J	A	S	O	N	D
Air (max)												
°C	16	16	18	21	24	28	30	39	28	26	21	19
°F	60	60	64	70	76	82	86	86	82	78	70	66
Air (min)												
°C	9	9	10	12	16	18	20	22	20	17	14	11
°F	48	48	50	54	60	64	68	72	68	62	57	52
Sea °												
C	16	16	17	18	20	23	24	25	24	23	19	17
°F	61	61	63	64	68	73	75	77	75	73	66	63

CLOTHING

Away from the beach, you should be fully clothed – Greeks take offence at bare or barely clad torsos of either gender. For sightseeing, bring shorts or lightweight trousers/dresses and T-shirts along with comfortable shoes for visiting archeological sites. When visiting churches or monasteries, men should wear trousers and women should wear trousers or skirts that cover the knees; and be sure to cover your shoulders and arms. For evenings, few places have a dress code, though smarter hotel dining-rooms require men to wear long trousers in the evenings and it's generally not de rigueur to wear sandals or flip-flops to dinner. If travelling in the mountains, note that sudden changes in weather require that you pack an extra layer or two.

CRIME AND SAFETY (See also Emergencies)

Crete is a relatively safe island to visit, with little major crime. However, petty crime and burglaries are on the increase so take precautions: leave valuables in your room safe and don't carry large amounts of cash around. If you are a crime victim, you will need to contact the local ordinary police in the first instance; insurance claims will not be valid without their paperwork.

D

DRIVING

Road conditions: Crete's roads have improved such that now only few parts of the island are inaccessible to a normal hire car. However, most roads have no paved shoulders, which can cause problems if you need to slow and leave the highway. Roads in the interior may be steep with hairpin turns – always allow extra time even for apparently short distances. You'll often encounter herds of goats and sheep using the roads too. In northern Crete there is a 'motorway' from Agios Nikolaos to Kastelli (Kissamos) via Heraklion, Rethymnon and Chania, corresponding to a UK dual carriageway. When it is finished, the A90, or BOAK, will be Greece's only motorway located on an island, connecting Kissamos with Sitia, a total length of approximately 300km.

Rules and regulations: Greece drives on the right and (theoretically) passes on the left. Yet Cretan drivers observe their own rules, often pulling over with no warning to talk to friends, driving on the wrong side of the road, or over-taking in any lane. The largest towns have one-way systems to ease the flow of traffic around the narrow streets, but many motorcyclists (and some car drivers) do not obey these rules. Always expect the unexpected and be aware.

Speed limits: 90km/h (56mph) on open roads and 50km/h (30mph) in towns, although most local drivers do not adhere to these speed limits and tailgate 'slowcoaches' mercilessly. Both speed-limit and distance signs are in kilometres. Seat belts are compulsory, as are crash helmets when riding a motorbike – non-observance will net you a draconian fine. Drink-driving laws are strict, and control points can test you and pull you off the road instantly. The acceptable alcohol level is 0.05 percent, and 0.02 percent for new drivers and motorcyclists.

Road signs: Signs often come late, hidden by vegetation or not at all, but where they do exist, are mostly international and easily understood, with names in both Roman script and Greek lettering.

Detour **ΠΑΡΑΚΑΨΗ Parákampsi**
Parking **ΠΑΡΚΙΓΚ Párking**
Forbidden **...ΑΠΑΓΟΡΕΥΕΤΑΙ ...apagorévete**
Be careful **ΠΡΟΣΟΧΗ Prosohí**
Stop **ΣΤΑΜΑΤΑ Stamáta**
For pedestrians **ΓΙΑ ΠΕΖΟΥΣ Gia pezoús**
Danger **ΚΙΝΔΙΝΟΣ Kíndinos**
No entry **ΑΠΑΓΟΡΕΥΕΤΑΙ Η ΕΙΣΟΔΟΣ Apagorévete i ísodos**

Fuel: Fuel in Crete is some of the most expensive in Greece, from around €2 per litre of unleaded 95 in towns, and more in remote areas. Petrol stations are reasonably common, but don't let your tank get too low, especially in the south. Most stations shut by 9pm, and many close on Sunday.

Parking: Although local drivers seem to park where they choose, there are enforced rules. Street parking is permissible, unless stated, but finding a space in towns can be a problem.

If you need help: Your car hire office should provide contact numbers for breakdown services. If you are involved in an accident with another vehicle, it is illegal to leave the scene – wait for the ordinary police or traffic police *(trohéa)* to show up and take statements.

> Fill the tank please, with (lead-free) petrol **Parakaló, gemíste i dexamení (me amólyvdi)**
> My car has broken down **To avtokínito mou éhi halási**

E

ELECTRICITY
The current in Crete is 230v/50Hz. Plugs and outlets are of the European continental two-prong type. Visitors from North America and the UK should bring plug adaptors, as well as dual-voltage shavers and hair dryers if required.

EMBASSIES AND CONSULATES
Australian Embassy and Consulate Hatziyianni Mexi Street 5, Level 2, 11528, Athens; tel: 21087 04000; www.greece.embassy.gov.au.
British Vice Consulate Candia Tower, Thalita 17, Iráklio; tel: 28102 24012; www.bit.ly/UKConsulCrete.
British Embassy and Consulate Ploutárhou 1, 106 75 Athens; tel: 21072 72600; www.gov.uk/world/greece.
Irish Embassy Vassiléos Konstandínou 7, 106 74 Athens; tel: 21072 32771; www.dfa.ie/irish-embassy/greece.
United States Embassy Vassiléos Sofías 91, 115 21 Athens; tel: 21072 12951; https://gr.usembassy.gov.

EMERGENCIES

Important telephone numbers:

General emergency phone number 112
Police (Emergency) 100
Ambulance 166
Fire brigade 199

G

GETTING THERE

By air: Greek airline Aegean (www.aegeanair.com), now incorporating Olympic Airlines, operates daily scheduled flights to Iráklio from Athens, Thessaloniki, Rhodes, and from Athens to Haniá. Sky Express (www.skyexpress.gr) offers flights from many Greek islands to Iráklio, as well as more unusual routes to Sitía. Book well in advance in summer.

Direct scheduled flights from the UK are operated by EasyJet (www.easyjet. com), TUI (www.tui.co.uk), Jet2 (www.jet2.com) and Ryanair (www.ryanair. com), but many visitors arrive on charter aircraft. A number of British tour operators offer flight-only or package deals from many UK airports; German, French, Italian and Swiss companies also fly in from around Europe.

By boat: There are daily car and passenger ferries from Athens (Piraeus) to Iráklio and Haniá, plus two a week between Kíssamos and the Peloponnese. Sailing time varies around 7–9 hours. The major companies are Minoan Lines (www.minoan. gr) and ANEK (www.anek.gr). Find up-to-date schedules at www.openseas.gr.

GUIDES AND TOURS

You can hire a personal, officially licensed guide to accompany you around Knossos; you will find them at the site entrance beyond the ticket office. For guides to other areas, the local tourist office will be able to provide you with details. Many taxi drivers are also happy to act as unofficial guides to their local areas.

Tour companies in every resort offer a variety of day trips by coach or boat, as well as more adventurous jeep safaris in the mountains. Most obviously, you can visit the archeological sites, Samariá Gorge, distant beaches and major towns of Crete from wherever you are staying on the island. Simply look out for the advertising boards.

H

HEALTH AND MEDICAL CARE

There are no vaccination requirements for your trip to Crete.

Emergency treatment is given free, although this only covers immediate needs. EU residents can get further free treatment with a European Health Insurance Card (EHIC; available online in Ireland from www.hse.ie) under reciprocal agreements. Since Brexit, UK citizens are entitled to free or reduced cost medical treatment on production of a Global Health Insurance Card (GHIC; apply for it online at www.bit.ly/GHICCard). Those in possession of a pre-Brexit EHIC still within its validity date can carry on using it until it expires. Nationals of other countries should check whether their government has a reciprocal health agreement, and/or ensure that they have adequate insurance cover.

It is highly advisable to take out additional travel insurance to cover you for protracted treatment or repatriation.

If you are taking any medication, bring enough for your holiday needs and keep it in its original packaging. If you have a basic medical need, look for a pharmacy, or *farmakío*, signified by a green cross, where you will be able to obtain advice and some medications can be bought over the counter. Most pharmacists speak some English.

Spiny sea urchins can cause serious injury if you step on or graze against them. Avoidance is the best option – they frequent rocky coasts with clean water; wearing swim shoes can help. A more common nuisance are mosquitos, so always use insect repellent in the evenings. Tap water is safe to drink, and indeed, is excellent in the Cretan mountains.

Dial 166 for 24-hour ambulance dispatch. Each major town in Crete has its own hospital with an emergency ward (*epígonda peristatiká*):

University General Hospital of Iráklio: Leof. Panepistimiou, Iráklio; tel: 28134 02111.

Ágios Nikólaos: on Knossoú opposite the Archaeological Museum; tel: 28413 43000.
Réthymno: on Triandalídou 19-21; tel: 28313 42100.
Haniá: in Mourniés district; tel: 28210 22000.

> a doctor/dentist **énas giatrós/odontogiatrós**
> hospital **nosokomío**
> an upset stomach **anakatoméno stomáhi**

L

LANGUAGE

Greek is not an easy language for English-speakers, but it is a beautiful one, and even a brief acquaintance will give you some idea of the debt western European languages owe to it. And the willingness to say even a few words will transform your status from that of *tourístas* to the honourable one of *kséno*, a word which can mean stranger, traveller and guest all rolled into one.

The sounds of the Greek language do not always correspond to exact equivalents in English, and the letters of the Greek alphabet do not always have a match in the Roman alphabet. This accounts for the divergent spellings of the same place name on Cretan road signs – for example, the word *ágios* is often also spelled *ághios* and *áyios* in the Roman alphabet, although it is always pronounced the same. Emphasis is also a vital element in pronouncing Greek. Throughout this book, we have accented vowels within each Greek word to show which syllable to stress. Most people working within the tourist industry will have a basic English vocabulary and many speak English very well.

The table lists the Greek letters in their upper- and lower-case forms, followed by the Roman letters used in this book to transcribe them, and a pronunciation guide.

A a	a	as in *fa*ther
B β	v	as in veto
Γ γ	g	as in *g*o (except before *i* and *e* sounds, when it's like the *y* in *y*es)
D d	d	sounds like *th* in *th*en
E e	e	as in *ge*t
Z ζ	z	same as in English
H η	i	as in *ski*
Φ θ	th	as in *th*in
I ι	i	as in *ski*
K κ	k	same as in English
Λ λ	l	same as in English
M μ	m	same as in English
N ν	n	same as in English
Ξ ξ	x	as in *box*
• o	o	as in *road*
Π π	p	same as in English
P ρ	r	same as in English
Σ σ,ς	s	as in *kiss*, except like *z* before *m* or *g* sounds
T τ	t	same as in English
Y υ	y	as in *country*
Φ φ	f	same as in English
X χ	h	rough, as in Scottish *loch*
Ψ ψ	ps	as in *tipsy*
Ω ω	o	as in *long*
ΑΙ αι	e	as in *hay*
ΑΥ αυ	av	as in *avant-garde*
ΕΙ ει	i	as in *ski*
ΕΥ ευ	ev	as in *ever*

ΟΙ	οι	i	as in *ski*
ΟΥ	ου	ou	as in *soup*
ΓΓ	γγ	ng	as in *longer*
ΓΚ	γκ	g	as in *gone*
ΓΞ	γξ	nx	as in *anxious*
ΜΠ	μπ	b or mb	as in *beg* or *compass*
ΜS	ντ	d or nd	as in *dog* or *under*

LGBTQ+ TRAVELLERS

Crete has no specific LGBTQ+ scene, but Haniá has long hosted a small community, and attitudes in the resorts are generally relaxed. Be discreet in the conservative rural communities. Homosexual practice is legal in Greece for people aged over 17 years old.

M

MAPS

Most maps of Crete are surprisingly inaccurate, with all showing the minor roads differently. Free maps from car hire companies are often no worse than commercial ones. Top touring coverage is provided by publisher Anavasi (www.anavasi.gr) based in Plaka, Athens; they also do the best topographical maps for hiking.

MEDIA

Newspapers: Major English newspapers can be bought in resorts one day after publication. Some English tabloids have European editions printed in Greece and available the same day. There is also the daily *Ekathimerini* (www.ekathimerini.com) included inside the *International Herald Tribune*.

Television and radio: Most hotels have satellite TV, which includes news channels such as CNN and BBC World. Many of the hotels also offer Netflix.

MONEY

Currency: The euro (€) is used in Greece. Notes are denominated in 5, 10, 20, 50, 100, 200 and 500 euros; coins in 1 and 2 euros and 1, 2, 5, 10, 20 and 50 cents, known as *leptá* in Greece. Notes of 100 euros and above are regarded with suspicion, as counterfeit, and will often have to be broken down in banks before you can use them.

Currency exchange: Most banks exchange foreign currency but charge a commission (usually 1–3 percent) for the service. Exchange rates appear on a digital display, and are generally the same for each bank. You can also change money at bureaux de change, found in many tourist centres and open longer hours than banks. Some advertise commission-free transactions, but exchange rates are often inferior to those of banks.

ATMs (cash machines): There are ATMs in every Cretan town or resort of over a few hundred inhabitants. These are the most convenient way to get euros.

Credit cards: Many hotels, restaurants, travel agencies and shops accept credit cards, but there is still a sizeable minority that do not, and out in the countryside credit cards are not generally accepted. Contactless payments are also becoming more common, although not accepted everywhere, and the maximum amount you can pay without entering a PIN is €50.

Travellers cheques: These are not recommended for use in Greece – expect severe delays or outright refusals in banks or bureaux.

O

OPENING TIMES

Opening times vary between official organisations and privately owned shops and cafés, and also between high and low season. Almost everybody closes mid-afternoon and official entities will not reopen later; if you need to get anything official done, do it in the morning.

Banks are open Monday–Thursday 8am–2.30pm, Fri 8am–2pm. Monday is a typical day of closure for museums, though major attractions will open daily (if perhaps only in the afternoon on Monday).

Shops are generally open Monday, Wednesday and Saturday 9am–2.30pm, closing at 2pm on Tuesday, Thursday and Friday, but open additionally 5.30–8.30pm. Supermarkets open Monday–Friday 9am–9pm, Saturday 9am–4pm; a very few may work Sunday 10am–4pm.

P

POLICE
Regular police officers wear two-toned blue uniforms. Tourist police (found in Iráklio, Haniá, Ágios Nikólaos and Hersónisos) also wear blue uniforms displaying a small national flag indicating which language they speak other than Greek. Main police stations are located as follows:
Iráklio: Agiou Artemiou Street 1; tel: 28102 74140.
Ágios Nikólaos: Erythroú Stavroú 47; tel: 28410 91413.
Réthymno: Iroon Politechniou 26; tel: 28310 88100.
Haniá: Iraklíou 23; tel: 28210 25700.

POST OFFICES
Post offices (7.30am–2pm) have blue-and-yellow livery, and are marked 'El-liniká Takhydromía' in Greek plus 'Hellenic Post' in English. Stamps can be bought here, or at postal agencies (usually small shops,) for a small premium. Packages for non-EU countries should not be sealed until they have been checked by post office staff.

Mail boxes are yellow – but be aware, in rural areas they are not emptied every day. Most hotels will post letters and postcards for you. Allow 4–7 days for postcards to Europe, 9–14 days for the rest of the world.

A stamp for this letter/ postcard **Éna grammatósimo gi'aftó to grámma/gi'aftí tin kart postál**

PUBLIC HOLIDAYS

Public holidays fall on the following dates:

1 January New Year's Day *(Protohroniá)*

6 January Epiphany *(Theofánia)*

25 March Greek Independence/Annunciation *(Evangelismós)* Day

1 May May Day

15 August Dormition *(Kímisis)* of the Virgin

28 October National *Óhi* ('No') Day

25 December Christmas *(Hristoúgena)*

26 December Gathering of the Virgin's Entourage *(Sýnaxis tis Panagías)*

Moveable dates: The first day of Lent (Clean Monday/*Katharí Deftéra*), Good Friday, Easter Monday and Whit Monday/*Agíou Pnévmatos*.

R

RELIGION

The population is almost 100 percent Greek Orthodox. However, Roman Catholic churches hold regular masses at Iráklio, Ágios Nikólaos, Haniá and Réthymno. There is a sizable Armenian community with its own church in Iráklio, and the Haniá synagogue conducts Friday evening services.

T

TELEPHONES

Since deregulation of the local telecoms market, a number of providers offer competition to the state-run OTE. OTE still, however, maintains most of the increasingly scarce public booths. Kiosks and newsagents sell OTE calling-cards in various unit denomination, as well as other products (including discount long-distance cards and local mobile top-up cards).

Most hotels of two-star rating and above have direct-dial lines, but add a huge surcharge to the cost of calls. Avoid this by using a prepaid, 12-digit-code card with an access number.

Foreign visitors with mobiles can also roam on one of the three Greek networks: Cosmote (www.cosmote.gr), Vodafone (www.vodafone.gr) and Wind (www.wind.gr). For visitors from the UK – since leaving the EU – and other non-EU nationalities, you'll need to check with your provider whether there are roaming fees for using your phone abroad (including texts and data services), or you could go home to a very hefty bill.

If you are staying more than a week or two, it might make sense to buy a local SIM with some talk-time and a data package included. It must be registered at time of purchase, but the number remains valid for a year from each top-up. Make sure your phone is unlocked to accept other SIM cards.

The international code for Greece is 30. Within Greece, all phone numbers have ten digits; fixed lines begin with 2, mobiles with 6.

TIME ZONES

Greece is two hours ahead of Greenwich Mean Time and also observes Daylight Savings along with the rest of Europe (but not the USA), moving clocks one hour forward between the last Sunday in March and the last Sunday in October.

In August, here is the time in the following cities:

New York	London	Jo'burg	**Crete**	Sydney
5am	10am	11am	**noon**	7pm

TIPPING

Service is notionally included in restaurant bills, although it is customary to leave between 5 and 10 percent of the bill in small change on the table. Hotel chambermaids should be left a tip of around €1 per day.

TOILETS

Large towns will have public toilets, usually near the marketplace or bus station. If attended, there is usually a €0.50 fee to the warden. Most museums have good public facilities.

Older sewage pipes in Greece are narrower than in most European countries and are easily clogged. Never put toilet paper into the toilet – always use the waste bin provided.

TOURIST INFORMATION

The Greek National Tourist Organisation, or Ellinikós Organismós Tourismoú (EOT; www.visitgreece.gr), is responsible for producing and dispersing tourist information. For information before you travel to Greece, contact one of the following offices:

Australia: 37–49 Pitt Street, Sydney, NSW; tel: (2) 9241 1663.

UK and Ireland: 5th floor east, Great Portland House, 4 Great Portland Street, London, W1W 8QJ, tel: (020) 7495 9300.

US: 305 East 47th Street, New York, NY 10017; tel: (212) 421 5777.

For local tourist information on the island, contact one of the following addresses:

Ágios Nikólaos: Aktí Koundoúrou; tel: 28410 22357.

Haniá: Kydonías 29, inside the city hall; tel: 28213 41665; www.chaniatourism.com.

Iráklio: Agiou Titou 1; tel: 2813 409000; www.heraklion.gr.

Réthymno: Delfini Building, Sofoklí Venizélou, town beach; tel: 28310 56350; www.rethymno.gr.

Another useful source of information is the Visit Greece app from the Greece National Tourist Office.

TRANSPORT

Buses: An excellent network of affordable bus services crosses the island, with stops at all the major archeological sites. Always arrive ahead of departure time. Tickets are bought on the bus or in advance. Iráklio has two bus stations: on the main road by the ferry port for north-coast services, outside the Haniá Gate for towards Phaistos, Mátala and Agía Galíni. Réthymno bus station is west of the town centre just off the coast road; Haniá's is centrally located on Kydonías, and in Ágios Nikólaos some way out near the Archaeological Museum. For up-to-date timetables and further information on travelling by bus, visit the website www.rethymnoatcrete.com/bus.htm.

Taxis: Taxis are numerous, and fares are regulated, but with surcharges for baggage and serving airports. They should have working meters that are set upon departure (to €1.20, not zero; minimum fare €3.20). Agree on hourly or daily rates before you set off.

Boats: Many resort ports are home to seasonal excursion boats, while various south-coast settlements are better connected by scheduled ferry services than by road. The main towns for taking boat trips are Ágios Nikólaos, Agía Galíni and Haniá, while daily ferries ply between Hóra Sfakíon, Loutró, Soúgia and Paleóhora.

> What's the fare to… ? **Póso éhi éna isitírio giá…?**
> When's the next bus to… ? **Póte févgi to epómeno leoforío giá…?**

V

VISAS AND ENTRY REQUIREMENTS

European Union (EU) citizens may enter Greece for an unlimited length of time. Citizens of the UK, the US, Canada, Australia and New Zealand can stay for up to 90 days within any 180-day period upon production of a valid passport; no advance visas are needed. From November 2023, UK citizens will require an ETIAS visa waiver, more information can be found here: bit.ly/ETIASUK.

Citizens of Ireland can enter the island of Crete with a valid identity card or passport. South African citizens require a Schengen Visa, which must be applied for in advance at the nearest Greek embassy or consulate in your home country.

There are no limits on the amount of hard currency visitors can import to Crete or export from the island, though amounts in excess of €10,000 equivalent should be declared.

WEBSITES

www.incrediblecrete.com Region of Crete's website on the island's attractions
http://visitgreece.gr Greece's official tourist website
www.explorecrete.com Useful general site with all sorts of info and links
www.climbincrete.com One-stop resource for trekkers and rockclimbers
www.chaniatourism.com Municipality of Haniá's website devoted to tourism
www.heraklion.gr Municipality of Iráklio's website
www.rethymno.gr Official website of Réthymno
www.west-crete.com Labour of love, with plenty of useful links, on all things found west of Réthymno

YOUTH HOSTELS

There are a number of youth hostels in Crete, including one in Haniá, one in Réthymno and one in Iráklio. None are members of the official youth hostel movement. You can book them at websites such as www.hostels.com. Each hostel, apart from the one in Iráklio has its own site:

Youth Hostel Plakiás: www.yhplakias.com
Réthymno Youth Hostel: www.yhrethymno.com
Cocoon City Hostel, Haniá: www.cocooncityhostel.com

WHERE TO STAY

Hotels in Greece are officially rated by EOT according to the facilities available. The former system of De Luxe, A, B, C, D and E class is replaced by a 5-to-no-star categorisation.

Accommodation in private rooms or apartments is graded from one to three 'keys'. In every room you'll find an official price placard on the back of the door. You should never pay more than this, and, except during the busiest seasons – Easter week, plus June through to September – prices ought to be significantly less.

Hotel booking websites can yield significant discounts at any time. Establishments below are open all year unless otherwise stated.

To dial the telephone numbers below from outside Greece you'll need to add the international country code +30. Prices are for a double room per night in high season.

€€€€€	over 170 euros
€€€€	120–170 euros
€€€	80–120 euros
€€	50–80 euros
€	50 euros and under

IRÁKLIO AND CENTRAL CRETE

Eva Marina € *Mátala resort,* www.evamarina.com. Small, 1980s vintage hotel, with pine furniture and white tiles underfoot, set in lush gardens, a short distance from the sea. Features an on-site hairdresser and sun deck. Each room has a patio and balcony and most face the garden. Open April–Oct. 20 rooms.

Galaxy Hotel €€€€ *Dimokratías 75, 71 306 Iráklio,* www.galaxy-hotel.com. The city's finest hotel offers grand public spaces and willing service. Interior-facing rooms are quieter, and guests lose nothing as regards the view. Facilities include a large pool, gym and hammam (steam room), restaurant and two bars (one poolside). 127 rooms.

Intra Muros Boutique Hostel € *Monís Kardhiotíssis 30, 712 01 Iráklio, tel: 6975 852 889,* www.intramuroshostel.com. One of two excellent back-packer-style hostels in Iráklio, offering mixed four- and 12-bunk rooms, a female-only six-bed dorm and a tiny, shared-bathroom double. The bunks are curtained off for privacy, there are lockers (bring your own padlock), and well kitted-out kitchen and shower facilities, plus a communal roof terrace with good views and a great traveller atmosphere. Located slightly out of the way, but in a quiet neighbourhood within easy walking distance of the town centre.

Kronos € *Agárthou 2, 712 02 Iráklio, tel: 2810 282 240,* www.kronoshotel.gr. This two-star hotel has a fabulous location by the central seafront, though the busy surrounding streets can mean some traffic noise. The en-suite rooms have a/c, TV, fridge and balcony, some with wonderful sea views (at extra cost).

Lato €€€€ *Epimenídou 15, 712 02 Iráklio,* www.lato.gr. Iráklio's first self-styled boutique hotel, with the best balconied rooms or suites facing the Venetian harbour (singles are very small). Walkable to all attractions yet reasonably quiet at night.

Marin Dream €€€ *Epimenídou 46, 712 02 Iráklio,* www.marinhotel.gr. Another boutique hotel with sweeping port views from the spacious front rooms – again, singles are tiny. A good breakfast is provided at the roof restaurant (not otherwise recommended). 43 rooms.

Olive Green € *Idhomonéos 22, 712 02 Iráklio, tel: 2810 302 900,* www.olive-greenhotel.com. Classy and very comfortable modern hotel that claims to be both ecofriendly and hightech (every room has a tablet to control lighting, a/c, etc). The beautifully designed rooms have powerful showers separate from the sink and loo. Impressive buffet breakfast included.

Villa Kynthia €€€€€ *Pánormos resort,* www.villakynthia.gr. A beautifully renovated, personably managed 1890s mansion-inn in this coastal village between Iráklio and Réthymno. Each of five units (2 rooms, 2 suites, 1 apartment) is individually furnished with antiques; common areas comprise a courtyard with small pool, breakfast lounge and bar.

ÁGIOS NIKÓLAOS AND THE EAST

Big Blue €€€ *west edge of town, by Roman cistern, 720 56 Mýrtos,* www.big-blue.gr. Choose from three grades of lodging at this ecologically-run complex with the best views in this resort. Breakfast served in terrace garden; extremely knowledgeable proprietor. 4 rooms, 6 studios and 2 apartments.

Du Lac €€€ *28 Octovriou str 17, 721 00 Ágios Nikólaos,* www.dulachotel.gr. Right beside Lake Voulisméni in the heart of the action, the excellent-value *Du Lac* offers a mix of designer-decor rooms and studios (the latter effectively 1-bed apartments), half of which overlook the water. Convenient ground-floor restaurant and café. 24 rooms.

El Greco € *Gavriil Arkadíou 13, 723 00 Sitía,* www.elgreco-sitia.gr. Best-value and friendliest hotel in the town centre, good views from the higher rooms and a pleasant lobby. Only downside is the tricky street parking.

Eloúnda Mare €€€€€ *720 53 Eloúnda,* www.eloundamare.com. The ultimate luxurious stablemate of the co-managed *Porto Elounda* complex (many facilities are shared), the *Elounda Mare* strikes a warmer, more intimate note, especially in bungalows and bungalow-suites with fireplaces, wood floors and private sea-water pools. The multi-levelled lounge and common areas continue outside as lovely terraced grounds lead down to stone lidos – there's little real beach here. Open late-April to late-Oct.

Istron Bay €€€€ *Istron, 721 00 Ágios Nikólaos,* www.istronbay.gr. Some 13km (8 miles) southeast of Ágios Nikólaos, this old-fashioned hillside complex remains competitive by dominating one of the area's best beaches. Among four grades of accommodation, choose superior standard or above. Open April–Oct.

Kakkos Bay €€€ *Koutsounári, 9km (6 miles) east of Ierápetra,* www.kakkosbay.com. 1980s-vintage but very pleasant resort scattered amidst well-tended gardens, pines and olive trees. Spacious bungalows (preferable to standard rooms) resembling Cretan country chapels from outside. A pool with all-day restaurant seems superfluous, since the complex brackets one of the calmest sandy coves in the region, sheltered from prevailing winds. Open May–Oct. 33 standard rooms, 27 bungalows.

Knossos Royal €€€€€ *700 14 Liménas Hersoníssou*, www.aldaemar-resorts.gr. This self-contained resort features low-rise units in three grades scattered across a large verdant plot. Family-friendly amenities include pools, restaurants, bars, shops, a kids' club, tennis courts and watersports. Guests can book treatments at the adjacent Aldemar Thalasso Spa. 364 units.

Marina Village €€ *behind Koureménos beach, 723 00 Palékastro*, www.marinavillage.gr. The three small wings of this 1980s hotel are idyllically set in olive groves and orchards, if a bit hard to find (follow the signs). Common areas include a pool, tennis court, bar and shady breakfast gazebo. Open April–Oct.

St Nicolas Bay Resort Hotel and Villas €€€€€ *721 00 Ágios Nikólaos*, www.stnicolasbay.gr. On the Nisí peninsula overlooking Mirabéllo Bay 1.5km (1 mile) north of town, this stone-clad resort offers discreet luxury with a degree of privacy for its suite-sized standard rooms, superior suites with private infinity pools, and a cluster of 3-or-4-bedroom villas with a private lido. Sandy coastline is limited to one small cove, but there's a full watersports programme and 34ft sailing boat to charter. A spa, kids' club and several (pricey) restaurants complete the picture. 107 units. Open April–Oct.

Stella's Traditional Apartments €€ *Káto Zákros, 72300 Sitía*, www.stelapts.com. Looking down over the local oasis to the eastern edge of Crete, these comfortable apartments are set in lush terrace-gardens with hammocks. There's spring water on tap and a sense of complete peace.

RÉTHYMNO, HANIÁ AND THE WEST

Anna's House €€€€ *300m/yds across river bridge, en route Vámos, Georgioúpoli*, www.annashouse.gr. More accurately, Anna's houses (plural) comprises of four grades of rooms, spacious apartments and villas, in landscaped grounds around a large pool. Open mid-March to mid-Nov.

Casa Delfino €€€€€ *Theofánous 9, Tophanás, 731 00 Haniá*, www.casadelfino.com. High-quality hotel where designer fittings are juxtaposed with recycled timber. The premises have been renovated by a descendent of the 19th century Genoese Delfino family who originally built this mansion. Differing units all have handmade Italian furniture and marble or solid wood flooring. There is also a spa and roof-terrrace bar. 20 suites, 4 standard rooms.

Doma €€€ *El. Venizélou 124, Halépa, 731 33 Haniá,* www.hotel-doma.gr. This converted neo-Classical mansion was once the Austro-Hungarian, then British Consulate. Now it's one of the gems of Crete, neither stuffy or luxurious, but appealing to those who want a low-key yet personal stay recalling the genteel old days. The dining room serves Cretan specialities for breakfast and pre-booked dinner. Open April–Oct. 25 units.

Fortezza €€€ *Melissinoú 16, 741 00 Réthymno,* www.fortezza.gr. This modern yet stylish hotel on the north side of the old quarter, just below the Venetian fortress, is handy for the town centre and waterfront, but still quiet. Its comfortable, air-conditioned rooms represent great value and there is medium-sized pool in the courtyard. 50 rooms, 3 suites.

Heracles € *Mitropolitou Isidorou 39, 740 53 Spíli,* www.heracles-hotel.eu. The quietest and best-run of three extant lodgings in this mountain town, Heracles has well-kept balconied rooms with bug-screens; the owner is a mine of information about the area. Breakfast isn't included. Bicycles can be rented. 5 rooms.

Milia Mountain Retreat €€€ *Vlátos, 730 12 Kissamos.* This eco-lodge is nestled in the hills of western Crete, off a secondary road between Kíssamos and Paleóhora. Old stone cottages of different sizes (2–4 persons) have open fireplaces for cool nights. An excellent affiliated taverna serves up three meals daily, based on local produce. By day, you can hike through nearby gorges or take painting courses; nights are spent gazing at the stars. 13 units.

Porto del Colombo €€€ *Theofánous & Moschon Corner, Tophanás, 731 10 Haniá,* www.portodelcolombo.gr. This historic Venetian mansion is now a luxurious inn, completely refurbished in mock-medieval style. Rooms are large, especially the galleried maisonettes, with carved-wood furniture and coloured tiles, plus proper shower stalls in the bathrooms. There are also 2-bedroom apartments adjacent. 10 rooms, 3 apartments.

Porto Loutro €€ *Loutró,* www.hotelportoloutro.com. Vehicle-free Loutró is accessible only by boat or on foot, so is wonderfully peaceful at night. This is the best hotel here, though still zen-minimalist. Two white-painted wings shelter standard rooms and studios with beamed ceilings and slate or marble flooring. The big attraction is taking in the sea view and slowing down to a local pace from your balcony. Cash only.

Theresa €€ *Angélou 8, Tophanás, 731 00 Haniá, tel: 28210 92798*. This characterful, budget pension has en-suite, often galleried rooms, accessed by a serpentine wooden staircase; the best are on the first floor. If you arrive and reception is unattended, simply check yourself in. There's a small kitchen, and roof terrace for great views over the harbour. Breakfast is available at the café next door. 7 rooms, plus a private house for guests who want intimate lodgings.

Vámos €€ *730 08 Vámos (midway between Réthymno and Haniá), Apokoronou*, www.vamosvillage.gr. Restored, stone-built houses scattered through Vámos old town, just 20 minutes from the sea. Most are maisonettes, with bedroom and bath upstairs, fireplace-lounges downstairs. Accommodation ranges from 2-person apartments to houses suitable for up to 8, with private or shared pool. There's an affiliated taverna, self-guiding walks and gastronomy classes held in an abandoned olive mill. 20 units.

Vecchio € *Daliáni 4, 741 00 Rethymno*, www.vecchio.gr. Hidden away in a narrow alley near the Rimóndi fountain, this Venetian mansion was one of the city's first boutique hotels, and is a serene haven. Balcony rooms are set around a courtyard pool; they're showing their age, but this is reflected in the price.

Veneto €€€€ *Epimenídou 2–4, 741 00 Réthymno, tel: 28310 56634*, www.veneto.gr. This is one of the better inns occupying 14th-century Venetian buildings in the old quarter, with an acclaimed in-house restaurant (half-board rates given). Public areas – including a large, arcaded courtyard with three potable springs, where breakfast is served – somewhat overshadow the rooms; upper-storey ones are airier and balconied. 12 suites.

Zafiri 2 €€ *Epar.Od. Strovlon-Paleochoras 28, 730 01 Paleóhora, tel: 28230 41811*. Studios and apartments on a quiet lane, with spacious, pleasant bedsit areas and long, narrow balconies affording limited sea views, though bathrooms are dated. The USP is the vast front lawn-garden where guests take their breakfast. 7 studios, 4 apartments.

INDEX

W
websites 135
White Mountains 83

X
Xylóskala 83

Y
youth hostels 135

Z
Zákros 65
   Palace of Zákros 65
Zarós 45

THE **MINI** ROUGH GUIDE TO
CRETE

First edition 2023

Editor: Annie Warren
Copy Editor: Tim Binks
Author: Rebecca Hall
Picture Editor: Tom Smyth
Cartography Update: Katie Bennett
Layout: Grzegorz Madejak
Head of DTP and Pre-Press: Katie Bennett
Head of Publishing: Kate Drynan
Photography Credits: 123RF 19; Bigstock 20, 68; Britta Jaschinski/Apa Publications 7T, 11, 32, 35, 37, 39, 40, 43, 47, 86, 88, 95, 107; Dreamstime 12, 85; Fotolia 65, 66, 70, 75; Georgios Tsichlis/Shutterstock 5T, 5M, 6T; GNTO 77, 81, 97; iStock 14, 22, 24, 30, 45, 48, 51, 53, 55, 57, 58, 61, 62, 73, 79, 82, 90, 93, 99, 103, 109; Shutterstock 1, 4ML, 4TL, 4ML, 5T, 5M, 5M, 5M, 5T, 6B, 7B, 17, 27; Yadid Levy/Apa Publications 104
Cover Credits: Frangokastello **Georgios Tsichlis/Shutterstock**

Distribution
UK, Ireland and Europe: Apa Publications (UK) Ltd; sales@roughguides.com
United States and Canada: Ingram Publisher Services; ips@ingramcontent.com
Australia and New Zealand: Booktopia; retailer@booktopia.com.au
Worldwide: Apa Publications (UK) Ltd; sales@roughguides.com

Special Sales, Content Licensing and CoPublishing
Rough Guides can be purchased in bulk quantities at discounted prices. We can create special editions, personalised jackets and corporate imprints tailored to your needs. sales@roughguides.com; http://roughguides.com

Contact us
Every effort has been made to provide accurate information in this publication, but changes are inevitable. The publisher cannot be held responsible for any resulting loss, inconvenience or injury sustained by any traveller as a result of information or advice contained in the guide. We would appreciate it if readers would call our attention to any errors or outdated information, or if you feel we've left something out. Please send your comments with the subject line "Rough Guide Mini Crete Update" to mail@uk.roughguides.com.